True Crime Stories of UPSTATE SOUTH CAROLINA

CATHY PICKENS

THE
History
PRESS

Published by The History Press
Charleston, SC
www.historypress.com

First published 2022

Manufactured in the United States

ISBN 9781467150767

Library of Congress Control Number: 2022933371

Notice: The information in this book is true and complete to the best of our knowledge. It is offered without guarantee on the part of the author or The History Press. The author and The History Press disclaim all liability in connection with the use of this book.

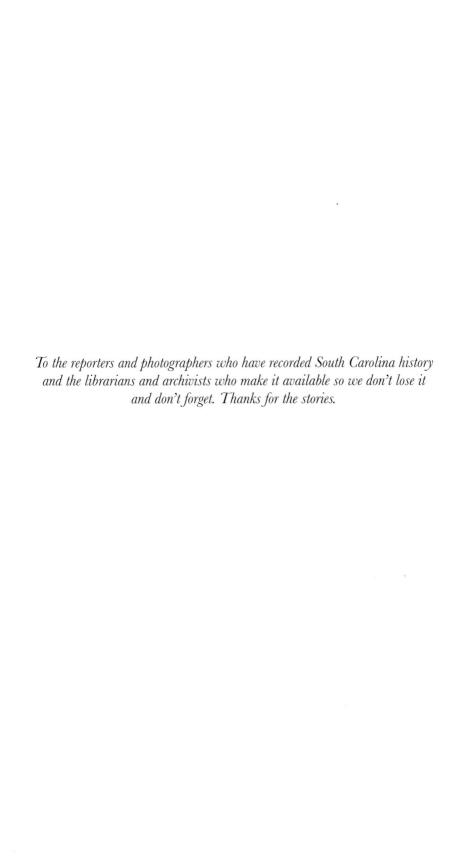

To the reporters and photographers who have recorded South Carolina history and the librarians and archivists who make it available so we don't lose it and don't forget. Thanks for the stories.

CONTENTS

ACKNOWLEDGEMENTS

Many thanks to:

Ashton Hester, former *Keowee Courier* editor and Walhalla's unofficial history consultant (see his Facebook history posts at https://www.facebook.com/ashton.hester.505).

John Lucas, Walhalla's unofficial murder expert.

Karl E. Addis, coroner, Oconee County, for providing long-ago inquest reports.

Dr. Will Sparks, who drove me to the Gaffney Library to introduce me to the Gaffney Strangler years ago.

Paul Anderson and his computer full of dead people.

Keith Vincent and his historic courthouse postcard site: www.courthousehistory.com.

Friend and professional photographer Andy Hunter. For traditional and drone photography, contact andyhunterphotos@gmail.com.

Mark Conrad (or "Detective Columbo") at Columbo's Pizza in Clemson, who told me the story I couldn't write…yet.

Margaret Dunlap and the Richland Library's Local History collection—pictures *do* tell the story.

Oconee County Library, which allowed me to be the first post-COVID visitor to its history collection.

Jack Grooms and his photographic assistance.

My writer friends and family, who always lend their advice, support and storytellers' eyes: Paula Connolly, Dawn Cotter, Terry Hoover, John Jeter and Ann Wicker. And Bob, expert at so many things, who is along for every adventure.

Chapter 1

WELCOME

Upstate South Carolina, the region known in the 1700s as the Backcountry, was very different from the coastal areas settled around Charleston—more subsistence farming than plantations, more independent Scots-Irish than class-conscious English. Stretching from the Chattooga River—the scenic, wild river bordering Georgia where the movie *Deliverance* was filmed—to the rich farmlands where tobacco has been replaced by turf farms, the region now boasts international business headquarters and universities along with rugged outdoor recreation destinations.

The stories in this book explore several decades of crime—cold-case murders, family betrayals, new-tech sleuths, a made-for-TV prison break, the state's more-than-fair share of serial killers and some unusual South Carolina poisoners—and range from the Piedmont cities into hill country, from nineteenth-century moonshiners to modern forensics, from international headlines to the little known.

My family has been in the Carolinas—in the Upstate—more than three hundred years. Any telling naturally depends on the storyteller's choices; these are cases that, for one reason or another, captured my imagination.

This book is not a work of investigative journalism. The information is drawn solely from published or broadcast resources, such as newspapers, television documentaries, podcasts, books, scholarly papers and print and online magazine articles.

One of the handicaps in recounting historical events is that accounts vary. Some reported "facts" aren't accurate—or they're at odds with someone

Reedy River Park in downtown Greenville contrasts the region's textile mill history and its modern growth. *Photo by Emmy Gaddy on Unsplash.com.*

else's memory or perception of the event. While I have worked to dig out as many points of view as I could find, I'm sure there are mistakes. My apologies in advance.

For me, what fascinates is not random violence but people, their lives, their relationships. Some of these stories could have happened anywhere. Some made huge headlines far away from South Carolina. Others remain writ large mostly in the hearts of the family and friends of those involved.

The stories, woven together, demonstrate the rich variety of those who call this part of the state home, the importance of family and friends, the contrasts of small towns and old farms nestled among cities. These are stories that have helped shape this part of South Carolina. People and their pasts matter here. The stories are worth remembering, even when they involve loss and especially when they are tempered with affection and fond memories.

Welcome to the upper region of South Carolina and its crime stories.

Chapter 2

THE POISONERS

South Carolina must cede to the state of North Carolina the title for most notorious female serial poisoners, with its well-known names like Velma Barfield and Blanche Taylor Moore and the less famous Sylvia White and Nannie Doss. Among the Upstate's few poisoners, one was caught after her first effort, and one was only in the Upstate to attend Clemson. The Upstate also had a not-quite-successful would-be poisoner—and one "victim" who was not poisoned at all. In those cases, no one died, but some interesting law was made.

Poison is usually considered a woman's weapon, though the homicide statistics can be misleading. Men commit 93 percent of murders. But when poison is the weapon of choice, the statistics take an interesting turn: poison is an equal-opportunity weapon. So, combining how rarely women kill and how often they choose poison, poison is indeed a woman's weapon—subtle, done at a distance of space and time by someone who has easy, close access to the victim.

Poison is a painful way to die and is not always predictable in its outcome. So, what kind of person chooses to inflict such a death? Ironically, statistics show poisoners tend to be caregivers—either family members or physicians and nurses. Poison is not usually an anonymous weapon; most poisoners kill someone they know.

Psychological evaluations indicate poisoners generally are self-centered manipulators who crave control but try to avoid confrontation. Poisoners are usually crafty, careful planners set on getting their own way, and they lack empathy for the suffering of others. If a poisoner is successful in her first attempt, she tends to gain confidence in her ability to pull it off again.

According to the national statistics, both current and across time, poison is a rarely used method of homicide. The more sobering statistic is that law enforcement has no idea how many cases go undetected. Even given dramatic improvements in toxicology testing, one out of five poison cases may remain unsolved. Even more sobering are the estimates that identified cases may be only a fraction of the actual number of homicidal poisoning deaths. Poison and poisoners are tricky indeed—and those in Upstate South Carolina are no exception.

PARIS GREEN

In 1924, Lillie Belle Griffin, convicted of attempting to poison her Greenville County neighbor, appealed to the state supreme court. The two neighbors had a history of "unpleasant relations." To settle their differences, Lillie Belle reportedly went to her neighbor's garden and sprinkled Paris green, an arsenic compound, over the turnip leaves, then traipsed through the potato patch on the way to her own back porch, leaving shoeprints in the soft dirt.

Paris green is a highly toxic powder, invented in 1814 as a distinctive dusky emerald paint pigment. By the late 1800s, farmers had found it made an effective poison for worms and bugs, even though it came as a tin of powder and was difficult to mix in water to spray on crops.

At Lillie Belle's felony trial, the sheriff testified that he'd tried to get her to step into one of the potato-patch shoeprints, but she refused. Or she wouldn't do it "the right way." So the sheriff "made her sit down on the grass, and take off her shoe; it fitted the track, presumably being adjusted by the sheriff."

With the help of the shoeprint evidence, the jury found Lillie Belle guilty of trying to poison her neighbor. In the appeal, no mention was made of whether Paris green would have been poisonous after the turnip greens were washed and cooked, whether rain could wash it off the leaves or whether it would be absorbed into the turnips and remain toxic. None of the toxicological details were explored because she was charged only with *attempting* to poison her neighbor.

Lillie Belle's appeal was based on two points in the sheriff's testimony: Did the shoe fit because he'd forced it into the shoeprint? And should he be allowed to testify that "she would not do it in the right way," implying she was uncooperative and therefore must be guilty?

Greenville County courthouse, scene of Lillie Belle Griffin's 1924 trial and now home to M. Judson Booksellers, stands next to the old Poinsett Hotel (now the Westin). *Photo by Cathy Pickens.*

The appellate court combed through cases from Massachusetts and Maryland to Oklahoma and Iowa, examining a prisoner's constitutional right not to be compelled to incriminate herself with her shoe or any other item (a gun, blood, burglary tools, counterfeit money) that might be found on her person. The appellate court held, as had other courts, that officers can confiscate items when arresting someone and can use the items to help prove the case—"and the law will not be hypercritical as to the method by which they may be secured."

So the sheriff could have Lillie Belle sit in the grass and remove her shoe to be tested.

However, regarding the second question, about making her put her foot in the print in the dirt, the court found other cases in other jurisdictions, also involving shoes and shoeprints at crime scenes, that suggested forcing Lillie Belle to do that made her incriminate herself. So Lillie Belle Griffin's conviction was reversed and sent back for a new trial. No second trial is recorded.

Over the years, courts have continued to wrestle with the line between diligent investigation and protection against self-incrimination. Blood typing, DNA identification and hair and fingerprint comparisons are just a few of the investigative tools that weren't on the minds of the drafters of the U.S. Constitution. The proper way to make Lillie Belle step in a shoeprint in a potato patch? With her consent. Or a search warrant.

A POISON TONGUE

Marital difficulties are nothing new, but each couple's difficulties take their unique path. From the start of Julia Mae and Dean Smith's February 1927 marriage in Spartanburg, the road was rocky. According to a court report, "He led a wild, reckless, and dissipated life, sometimes at work, but frequently unemployed, and drifting from one place to another." The couple separated ten times in the first six years of their marriage.

But then Dean Smith saw the light and was converted at a church meeting in Pennsylvania. He became an ordained minister and, the next year, was pastoring two small Upstate churches.

At that seemingly positive point, the rift between the spouses grew wider. Dean wanted to go to school to further his ministerial career. He felt Julia Mae wasn't creating for him the peaceful, supportive home he needed. She "was not the kind of wife a minister should have," the court report said. But

Julia Mae felt differently about that. She'd stuck to the marriage through bad times. Now, Dean said, she'd given him an ultimatum: "I would live with her or I would not live with anybody."

Julia Mae had been staying in Spartanburg and working as a seamstress before she moved back to Chesnee, where Dean was preaching, to live with him for their latest attempt to reconcile. Things weren't working out, so, on December 18, 1934, he agreed to take her back to her mother's house.

That morning, as was his custom, Dean drank a quart of sweet milk—a term used to distinguish regular milk from buttermilk. Julia Mae refused his offer to share the milk, so he downed the whole quart before they left for Spartanburg.

Dean didn't make it back home to Chesnee before he began having "violent stomach pains." His doctor diagnosed ptomaine, or food poisoning, something he'd treated Dean Smith for three or four times in the past.

No matter what the doctor said, Dean believed his wife had poisoned him. He must have generously shared his belief with his parishioners, and a story that juicy was bound to spread quickly. Imagine learning the pastor's wife tried to poison him on her way out the door back to her mama's.

The rumors eventually made their way to Julia Mae, but trying to fight an accusation like that could just fan the flames, so she tried to ignore it. Four years later, the now-Reverend Dean Smith had a working relationship with the more experienced Reverend J. Harold Smith. The two men weren't related. Reverend Harold had stayed at Reverend Dean's house when he held a revival in Chesnee. While there, Reverend Harold learned from deacons and members at the Baptist church about why Reverend Dean no longer lived with his wife.

A broken home was a tarnish on the credibility of a minister, so Reverend Harold sought to reconcile the couple. Julia Mae agreed, and Reverend Harold gathered the couple to pray. Reverend Harold later said she was disrespectful to him during that reconciliation attempt. Other witnesses, though, said he exaggerated her reaction to his prayers.

In May 1938, Reverend Harold held a big service in Hendersonville, North Carolina. He invited several ministers, including Dean, to sit on the platform with him. During his sermon to some 1,500 people from all over the area, he pointed to Reverend Dean, sitting behind him on the stage, and told the congregation, "I don't blame him for not living with his wife; she poisoned him."

Reverend Harold said he wanted to explain to those in the congregation why Reverend Dean was a reputable man of God and worthy as a church leader.

That was Julia Mae's breaking point. She tried to get the preacher to retract his accusation. But the Reverend J. Harold Smith refused. What he said, he believed to be the truth; he said it to help Reverend Dean's ministry; and even Dr. Cash, Dean's physician, had said Dean was poisoned—or so Reverend Harold claimed.

When Julia Mae sued him for slander, Reverend Harold didn't have Dr. Cash to back him up. In fact, the doctor was upset that the preacher so blatantly misrepresented his diagnosis of food poisoning.

Julia Mae's lawsuit asked for actual and punitive damages. Slander is spoken defamation of character and is one of the few civil actions in which the plaintiff can be awarded punitive damages, designed to punish or make an example of the defendant for stepping beyond the bounds of ordinary negligence. The jury agreed with Julia and awarded her $425 in actual damages and $425 in punitive damages.

Years before he was elected governor, and later as a write-in candidate for the United States Senate, Strom Thurmond served as acting justice on the state appellate court that heard Reverend Harold's appeal. The court methodically evaluated the arguments and upheld Julia Mae's award, about $16,000 in today's dollars.

After the lawsuit, the Smiths disappeared from the headlines.

THE EYEDROP MURDER

On July 21, 2018, a man riding his motorcycle past a blue-gray York County house with soaring white columns stopped when a distraught woman ran across the lawn, flagging him down.

"Call 911!" Lana Clayton begged.

Lana then ran to a neighbor's house and banged on the door. The neighbor drove her back to her house in his golf cart.

Lana's sixty-four-year-old husband, Steven Clayton, lay at the bottom of the sweeping staircase. The neighbor could find no pulse.

Medics and firefighters arrived at the home in the quiet neighborhood bordering Lake Wylie to find Steven Clayton lying just inside the front door, dead. The address was Clover, South Carolina, though the house was closer to North Carolina than to either Clover or Rock Hill. First responders thought they were looking at a tragic accident—a fall down the stairs.

Police body camera footage shows the officers and the deputy coroner on the scene. Lana Clayton sat on the sofa, telling them her husband had been in bed for three days suffering a bout of vertigo. He must have tried to get up while she was outside doing yard work, she said. Those investigating the death were considerate of her grief.

Steven Clayton was a big man with a big personality. He and Lana, fifty-four, had been married five years. He'd retired in 1995 after building a national chain of physical therapy clinics. As a high school athlete, he competed in track, football and wrestling, and he coached high school wrestling for a time. Lana was a former Veterans Affairs nurse and a member of a local Bible study group. The couple was known for the parties they threw, filling their big house and yard with food, friends, music and dancing.

Steven Clayton had six ex-wives but no children of his own. Two nephews lived nearby, and he was close with his large extended family.

One of Steven's nephews, Nick French, came as soon as he got the news. When Nick arrived, he started looking at the scene with the skeptical eye of a police officer—which he was, in a nearby jurisdiction.

To Nick, what Lana was saying didn't make sense. She was a nurse. Why would she leave him in the bedroom, lying on a urine-soaked mattress? "That happens when he gets vertigo," was her only reply.

Why didn't Steven call for help? He was constantly on his cell phone, but no one had heard from him in days, and they couldn't find his phone anywhere in the house. Why had Lana not told them he was so sick?

Nick listened as the deputy coroner asked what funeral home Lana wanted to use. Lana just couldn't think about that, she said—but she quickly had another answer as soon as the deputy coroner said she could take the body to the morgue for tests.

Lana became angry when Nick decided to phone Steven's other nephew, Kris.

The next alarm bell sounded when Kris offered to help find Steven's will. Steven had asked Kris to be his executor. Lana said, "There is no will." But Kris knew there was; he had seen it.

The final alarm bell sounded when Lana explained why she didn't want Steven's body autopsied. She claimed he regularly abused illegal drugs, which probably caused a heart attack, and she didn't want his drug use made public. She sent his body to the mortuary with instructions that it be cremated.

No one in Steven's family believed Lana's stories of drug abuse—or much of anything else she said that day.

As a police officer, Nick knew who to call: Sabrina Gast, the York County coroner. She could order a postmortem exam.

The physical autopsy showed no clear reason for Steven's death: his heart was fine. The toxicology screen told a different story. When the neurotoxin tetrahydrozoline popped up on the printout, the investigators' questions got a lot more focused. Tetrahydrozoline is an ingredient in several non-prescription eyedrops. The coroner said Steven's body contained "poisonous levels" of the colorless, odorless, tasteless chemical at the time of his death.

Using eyedrops to make someone sick entered the popular culture conversation with the 2005 movie *Wedding Crashers*. As a joke, a character claims that putting eyedrops in someone's drink would cause diarrhea, thus getting a rival temporarily out of the way.

But a romantic comedy isn't the place to get reliable medical information. The movie left out the dangers of tetrahydrozoline. When used as intended, it eases eye redness by constricting the blood vessels. When taken internally, though, it causes the heart to race or the blood pressure to drop, along with nausea and vomiting, difficulty breathing, drowsiness, convulsions and, often, an odd mix of sleepiness and anxious hyperactivity. While most people who swallow it survive—sometimes after a trip to the hospital—it can cause death in less than thirty minutes.

Sometimes, the person squirting the bottle of eyedrops into a glass of water or a drink doesn't intend it as a joke. Sometimes, she knows exactly what she's doing.

What killed Steven Clayton was no longer the question. Now, investigators needed to know how he ended up drinking enough of the eyedrops to kill him.

Lana came to the sheriff's office to answer questions, but her answers shifted and varied as she began to realize the officers knew more than they were telling her. She said Steven had put eyedrops in his coffee every morning for years so he would have a bowel movement—a ridiculous claim, according to medical experts. She said he was demanding, abusive, a hard-core drug user—though family members and an ex-wife had seen no such behavior.

Finally, Lana admitted she had added the drops to the water glass by his bedside while he was sleeping. She admitted she wanted him to suffer. She claimed, despite her nursing background, that she didn't think it "was anything that would be serious to your, to your health," she told the officers. She didn't intend to kill him.

Digging deeper into the couple's background, they found plenty of friends who talked about how happy the two seemed together. But they also found an earlier police report. In May 2016, investigators questioned Lana after she shot Steven in the head with a crossbow. She said it was an accident, that she was trying to load the crossbow they kept in their bedroom when it fired, striking him in the back of the head as he slept. Fortunately, the arrow glanced off his skull, and the wound was not serious.

Steven believed it was an accident. No charges were filed, even though at the time, Lana complained to investigators of her husband's abusive mood swings.

The two continued to live together for two years.

Authorities began hearing from family members who had suspicions, especially about the missing will. The house was worth $1 million, Steven's other assets worth another million. Without a will providing for his family members, South Carolina law said Lana would inherit everything.

Another sinister coin dropped in the slot: Lana was the one who insisted the couple move from North Carolina to their South Carolina home in 2016—the same year as the crossbow incident. Some speculated whether the move had anything to do with what happened in South Carolina if someone dies without a will. But the inheritance laws don't differ significantly between the two states. So perhaps Lana thought law enforcement would be less professional in a more rural county? No one had clear answers to those questions, but the family couldn't help but wonder. Steven had always been the protective stalwart for his extended family—and now he was gone.

THE CLAYTON CASE MADE headlines worldwide, though it was not the only eyedrop poisoning case in the United States—not even the only one in the Carolinas. Poison Control reports over one hundred cases a year of dangerous exposure to eyedrops, mostly children accidentally drinking from a bottle left lying around the house. Two months after Steven Clayton's death, a woman in Mount Holly, North Carolina, died. A year later, a man in Salisbury, just north of Charlotte, was dead; his fiancée said she just wanted to make him sick. Were these copycat killings?

As with most poisonings, exact numbers of cases are hard to calculate. And motives are hard to discern.

In August, just weeks after Steven's death, authorities were again called to the Clayton home. Police smelled the odor of natural gas. Lana was inside, unconscious in the bed. She had written notes saying she felt bad about Steven and she didn't want to live with it anymore. She took pills and turned on the gas.

Lana recovered and was arrested the next day, August 31, charged with murder and malicious tampering with food with intent to cause harm. Both are felonies in South Carolina and could earn her the death penalty.

Rather than proceed to trial, Lana pled guilty in January 2020 before Judge Paul Burch. Excerpts from her statement to the judge were televised. She said she didn't mean to kill Steven; she just wanted to teach him a lesson about his verbal abuse.

The judge took sharp issue with that claim. "How can you maintain you did this to teach him a lesson, when it is obvious from the facts that you let him suffer for three days? You ignored him." The judge also pointed out it was obvious Lana had hidden his phone so he couldn't call for help. Furthermore, if she was being abused, she had the power to leave.

The prosecutor argued a likely motive: "Steven Clayton was worth a lot of money. She wanted his money."

In mitigation, Lana's defense attorneys pointed to two incidents of rape earlier in her life and to her reputation as a caring person.

Steven's family members said Lana had duped them for most of the five-year marriage. After Steven's death, they said, they began to recognize the incidents of manipulation and deviousness for what they were.

In a *48 Hours* interview, Steven's sister, Rosie Clayton-Leslie, said she told the judge she "knew it had to be very difficult to see someone who looks so frail, so gentle, so quiet and meek…and think that that person could be a cold-blooded murderer." She didn't want the judge to be fooled by the woman standing before him.

At sentencing, Judge Burch spoke directly to Lana: "This one takes the cake as far as being bizarre. The old saying, 'What a tangled web we weave.' Ms. Clayton, you sure have tangled this one up."

He sentenced her to twenty-five years in prison.

THE MENSA MURDER

Universities have good reason to celebrate their successful graduates, but alumni magazines don't tout the questionable accomplishments of their former students who turn what they learned to nefarious purposes. In the case of George J. Trepal, Clemson and the University of South Carolina have good reason to omit his extra-professional accomplishments from their alumni news.

When he was young, Trepal's parents moved with their only son from New York City to Florence, South Carolina. In 1966, Trepal graduated from McClenaghan High School (the building now houses Florence County education offices) and enrolled in Clemson that fall. Despite his near-genius

IQ, two years later, his grades were too low for him to return to Clemson. In 1969, he enrolled at USC and graduated in 1972 with a psychology degree. He moved to Charlotte that same year.

Trepal later married orthopedic surgeon Dr. Diana Carr, and in the early 1980s they moved to Alturas, a small town in central Florida east of Tampa. They chose a house amid the orange groves outside of town. The two enjoyed their membership in Mensa, an organization for people who measure in the top 2 percent in intelligence, and quickly became active with the Florida club.

They didn't, however, much enjoy their closest neighbors, especially after Parearlyn "Pye" Carr's new wife, Peggy, and her son moved into Pye's home in 1988. The blended household now consisted of Carr's son Travis, his daughters Delena and Tammy, granddaughter Kasey, and Peggy Carr's son Duane. The daughters lived in the garage apartment Pye had renovated for them.

With no neighbors other than the Trepals within a quarter mile, the family of seven enjoyed outdoor activities. Soon the Trepals' complaints about loud music, noisy ATVs and the Carrs' barking dogs chasing their cats turned into verbal altercations between Dr. Diana Carr and Peggy Carr. (No relation between the two.)

In June 1988, Pye got a disturbing anonymous letter—with his name misspelled as "Pie"—postmarked from nearby Bartow, Florida: "You and all your so-called family have two weeks to move out of Florida forever or else you will all die. This is no joke."

The family shrugged off the threat, figuring it was yet another bit of nonsense from their crazy neighbor.

In late October 1988, Peggy Carr became ill with nausea, chest pain, trouble breathing and needle-sharp pain in her hands and feet. After three days in the hospital, she felt well enough to return home, but then the symptoms returned—and started affecting the two sons. All three were admitted to the hospital.

Peggy began losing clumps of hair, which alerted her physician. Lab tests showed Peggy and the two teenagers had ingested varying levels of thallium.

One son stayed in the hospital for two months, the other for six months. Both recovered. Peggy survived in a coma for four months, but despite the doctor's best efforts, she died on March 3, 1989.

Thallium is a heavy-metal poison, toxic to humans in a relatively small dose: one gram or less for most people. It can be dissolved in liquid and is colorless and odorless. Dissolved in sweet liquid, thallium was once used as a rat poison, but because of its toxicity, it was banned from households in 1965 and commercially in 1975, with limited lab uses allowed.

Humans naturally ingest small amounts of thallium in their diet, with no ill effects. Larger doses, though, accumulate in the body and are expelled slowly. The painful, debilitating progress of a lethal dose can be tracked over several days as the effects build: mild aches like a cold or flu; gastric symptoms such as cramps, diarrhea and vomiting; intense body pain; increasing tingling and sensitivity in the feet and hands; insomnia; slurred speech; and finally, overall debility and death.

Through the 1930s, thallium was used as a pretreatment for ringworm because of its most distinctive side effect: hair loss. Unbeknownst to the parents who administered it to their children, hair loss signals a near-lethal dose of thallium. Because the early signs of thallium poisoning can mimic gastroenteritis or a severe flu, hair loss is often the clearest clue to medical personnel that they're dealing with a thallium poisoning case.

Thallium has been the weapon of choice in a few fictional murders, perhaps most famously—and most accurately—in Agatha Christie's *The Pale Horse*. Christie took the title from Revelation 6:8: "And I looked, and behold a pale horse: and his name that sat on him was Death, and Hell followed with him." Only much later would the investigators at the Carr house come to appreciate that the mystery novel's plot involves not just thallium but also voodoo and black magic.

While investigators from the sheriff's department, the state and local health departments and the federal Environmental Protection Agency worked to locate the source of the thallium, hospital doctors also found levels of the poison in Pye, one of his daughters and his granddaughter. Of the seven family members, only one daughter showed no signs of thallium exposure.

The source of the thallium at the Carr house was not easy to find. Technicians combed the house, searching everything from ice cubes to paint scrapings from the walls. The four hundred samples sent to the state lab included four empty sixteen-ounce glass Coca-Cola bottles. Those bottles yielded the answer: thallium residue. The three remaining full bottles of Coke retrieved from the house showed subtle signs that the caps had been removed and replaced, likely with a device designed to cap bottles. Those three bottles contained lethal and near-lethal amounts of thallium.

Police weren't surprised to learn that Peggy drank more of the Cokes than anyone, to settle her stomach when she first got sick. The daughter who had no symptoms didn't drink any Coke.

As part of their routine canvas of neighbors and friends, investigators questioned Trepal in December, while Peggy lay in a coma. When asked if he knew any reason why someone might want to poison the Carrs, Trepal said maybe to persuade them to move away. That odd answer got investigators' attention because it echoed the threat in the anonymous letter Pye received.

Despite their questions, investigators didn't have probable cause to search Trepal's house. As the leads began to dry up, the sheriff learned about a Mensa murder mystery weekend and asked Special Investigator Susan Goreck to attend the event undercover. She'd be able to fit in—and perhaps learn more about the odd neighbor.

Trepal and Goreck, using the name Sherry Guin, struck up a friendship over the next several months: taking hikes, visiting a museum, having picnics. Trepal was quiet, obviously intelligent, and dressed like a leftover hippie. He told people that he worked developing computer programs, but his wife was the breadwinner. He seemed to appreciate having an audience for his encyclopedic interests. Goreck found him sometimes fatherly.

When Goreck learned Trepal's wife wanted to move to Sebring, less than an hour away, to a new medical practice, Goreck asked Trepal if she could rent their Alturas home. As soon as the rental agreement was finalized and Trepal said they'd finished moving out, Goreck, local officers and an FBI agent entered the house and began their search, a year after first questioning Trepal.

In a workbench in Trepal's garage workshop, an officer found a brown bottle with a powder residue: thallium. In subsequent searches in Sebring, investigators also found a bottle-capping machine, chemistry lab equipment and a copy of Christie's *The Pale Horse* among a collection of mysteries.

Trepal owned several chemistry books with sections on thallium and had written a booklet on "Chemistry for the Complete Idiot, Practical Guide to all Chemistry," with illustrations and an index. He'd also compiled his own notebook, "A general poison guide," with pages photocopied from references that included a book titled *Poison Detection in Human Organs* and another with a section called "Death by Poison Synopsis." One of the books he photocopied came from the library at Central Piedmont Community College, where he attended pottery-making courses in 1974 and 1975 when he lived in Charlotte.

One passage from Trepal's journal said, "Determining whether a person died as a result of natural illness or as a result of poisoning is one of the most difficult types of investigation both for the officer and for the medical expert." Another said, "The presence of any one poison is so difficult to ascertain that it may be undetected unless the [medical] examiner has some idea as to the type of poison for which he is looking." Investigators tested the poison journal for fingerprints. They found George's but not Diana's.

At Trepal's trial, Diana Carr offered plausible explanations for much of what investigators found suspicious. Because of the events at Peggy and Pye Carr's house, materials Trepal had written for the Mensa murder weekend where Goreck first met Trepal sounded suspicious to investigators. But his wife said Trepal borrowed the material from Robert Tallant's classic 1946 book *Voodoo in New Orleans*: "I ain't afraid of no voodoo…but I am afraid of poison.…If they can get some of that in what you eat, it's too bad."

Dr. Carr and Trepal owned lots of books, she said. She was an avid mystery reader with hundreds of mysteries on her shelves, including Agatha Christie titles. "George had all kinds of books," she told *Orlando Sentinel* reporter Mike McLeod. "When we looked for a house we told the Realtor that was why we needed a lot of room. Not for us. For the books. He had books from Zen to auto mechanics. Saying George had books on poisoning is like saying the public library has books on poisoning."

Investigators knew Trepal earned a degree in psychology at the University of South Carolina. He also had a sophisticated applied knowledge of chemistry. He'd been arrested while living in Charlotte on charges that he was associated with of one of the largest methamphetamine manufacturing operations in North Carolina. The DEA agent who arrested him testified Trepal was the chemist and mastermind for that lab and said other dealers in the area knew of his reputation, even though he stayed behind the scenes.

After Trepal's 1978 release from his stint in North Carolina's federal prison at Butner, he met Diana, who was equally smart and bookish but more assertive. They moved to Florida when she finished her medical residency.

Given Trepal's chemistry background, his odd interview statement and the evidence found in his house, he was charged with first-degree murder, attempted murder and tampering with a consumer product. His monthlong trial started in January 1991.

The case made headlines as the "Mensa murder," not solely because Trepal was smart enough to be a member but also because he and his wife had hosted the local club's now-infamous Mensa murder weekend. Dr. Diana Carr, the lifelong lover of mystery novels, wrote the script for the role-playing murder mystery game designed to play out over a weekend at a local motel. The members assumed the various roles and tried to solve the four intricate puzzle mysteries. Each of the make-believe murders was presaged by an anonymous note.

A booklet Trepal wrote to accompany the role-playing scripts discussed poisons and threats from neighbors: "Few voodooists believe they can be killed by psychic means, but no one doubts that he can be poisoned. When a death threat appears on the doorstep, prudent people throw out all their food and watch what they eat. Hardly anyone dies from magic. Most items on the doorstep are just a neighbor's way of saying, 'I don't like you. Move or else.'"

To investigators, the booklet provided a window into how Trepal's mind worked.

The state's evidence included research done by the Coca-Cola Company. In tests using six common forms of thallium, the lab found only two of the forms could be added to a bottle of Coke without changing its color or causing it to foam out of the bottle, leaving behind a partially empty bottle. The thallium found in the bottle in Trepal's garage was one of those forms.

FBI profiler Bill Hagmaier, whose career included getting Ted Bundy's final confession, had advised the Trepal investigators since early in the case on the psychology of poisoners. While attending Trepal's trial, Susan Goreck asked the agent what would happen to her if the jury let Trepal go. After all, her undercover work led to critical evidence in the case. Hagmaier told her, "George doesn't get mad. He gets even."

The jury found Trepal guilty of first-degree murder and fourteen lesser charges—fifteen separate guilty verdicts.

In Trepal's long series of appeals in the Florida courts, he pointed the finger at Pye Carr, whom Peggy had confronted about having an affair; at police for allegedly planting the thallium bottle in his house and for incorrectly testing the contents of the bottle; and at the hospital physician for being the most direct "cause" of Peggy's death—not Trepal. Trepal also claimed the bottles of Coke had not been proven to contain deadly doses of poison. Trepal appealed again after an FBI report specifically cited Trepal's case in criticizing the work and testimony of a particular FBI agent. The Florida Supreme Court, in a lengthy 2003 review of the effect of that agent's testimony, again upheld Trepal's conviction.

Sentenced in March 1991, Trepal sits on death row in Florida's Union Correctional Institution (formerly Florida Prison and Raiford Prison). His wife remarried and continued her career as a much-honored orthopedic surgeon. She died in 2018.

Chapter 3

PRISON FLY-OUT

PERRY CORRECTIONAL

Love takes some people to crazy places, but Joyce Bailey Mattox's neighbors in Wellford, near Greenville, didn't expect anything as crazy as where love led the forty-year-old, thrice-divorced woman.

In 1985, Joyce had been writing letters to, then talking on the phone with, then visiting an inmate at Perry Correctional Institution in Pelzer, about forty miles from her home. She'd met Jesse Glenn Smith, thirty-six, through a connection she had with another inmate, though it isn't quite clear who introduced them. He was serving time for armed robbery, receiving stolen property and assault and battery with intent to kill.

Another inmate serving time for armed robbery, William Douglas Bellew, was perhaps a fan of prison-break movies. He came up with a plan and suggested it to Smith. It was a doozy: get a hijacked helicopter to fly into the prison yard and escape.

The crazy plan required somebody on the outside. After eight months of chaste kisses and hand-holding during monitored prison visits, Joyce was game to help with the scheme. With $780—all her available cash—she tried unsuccessfully to get neighbors to help her buy a gun. For protection against one of her ex-husbands, she said. Apparently her neighbors didn't want to get involved, because she ended up having to buy the gun on her own, at a pawnshop. The pawnshop employee loaded the .32-caliber handgun for her because she didn't know anything about guns.

Joyce's neighbors did help her drop her car off in a field not far from Perry Correctional and drop another car at a convenience store about twenty miles away from the field. Joyce told them she had friends who were coming to pick up the cars.

A neighbor then dropped her at Palmetto Helicopter. He later said her explanations and plans didn't make much sense, she just "talked in circles," but at the time, he shrugged it off. That was Joyce.

At Palmetto Helicopter, Joyce was greeted by Larry Green, a pilot who had earned plenty of hours flying in Vietnam. She wanted to take a sightseeing trip in his big copter, she said. Was she later disappointed that he talked her into the smaller two-seater copter? She probably didn't know at the time that it wouldn't easily do the job she needed done.

Green and Joyce took off in the smaller copter. She slipped the $165 flight fee into his pocket, in cash, pulled her .32 from the top of her cowboy boot and ordered him to fly to Perry Correctional. She also told him to remove his headset, which kept him from communicating with anyone. Somebody had done some homework.

At the prison, one guard routinely monitored from the tower while another guard drove the perimeter in a vehicle. As the copter approached the twelve-foot, razor-wire-topped fence, two hundred men were outside in the recreation yard enjoying the December day.

Green sat the copter down in the yard, as ordered. He wasn't about to argue with the lady waving the gun. In the ensuing confusion, Smith, Ballew and a twenty-year-old inmate named James Rodney Leonard knew what to do. They made a dash for the copter door. A guard chased them and tried to yank at least one of them from the door. The gun fired from inside the copter. A bullet hit the guard in the mouth, breaking his jaw and several teeth.

The mission lasted two minutes. Fortunately for Joyce and her other passengers, Green's military experience got the overweight helicopter over the fence and to the field five miles away where Joyce had parked her Chevy Nova. Leaving Green and his copter in the field, Smith drove off with Joyce as the other two men hid in the back seat. At the convenience store, they switched to the Dodge Aspen and took off, playing country music, drinking beer and eating fast food. On their first night of freedom, the other two escapees allowed Joyce and Smith some privacy at a hotel.

Entrance to Perry Correctional Institution in Pelzer, with a higher fence visible in the background. *Photo by Cathy Pickens.*

After checking those initial items off their list, the group seemed rather aimless. No clear plan about where to go or how to survive.

Back in Greenville, police weren't nearly so aimless. Joyce's abandoned car gave the police a name, which they broadcast widely, along with her picture and those of the escapees.

The quintet stole a Pontiac with Alabama license plates. They kept driving, but as things turned out, they were going nowhere particular and not very fast. Four days after the brazen escape, they'd made it as far as the Interstate 95 welcome center at the Florida-Georgia line—about 350 miles and only about five hours' driving time on the shortest route from Greenville.

At three thirty that morning, a state trooper cruising the rest area lot ran the stolen Pontiac's plates and called for backup. The sleepy getaway gang woke up facing armed officers with blinding flashlights.

Brought before a South Carolina court, Joyce faced state charges of assault and aiding and abetting escape. Since it was unclear who pulled the trigger in the prison yard, they all were charged with assault and battery with intent to kill for shooting the guard. Joyce also faced federal charges for air piracy, which carried a stiff penalty—forty years.

Smith and Ballew received life sentences for kidnapping, along with additional state and federal sentences. Leonard got additions to his existing sentence for accessory, conspiracy and escape. All three men got lengthy federal extensions to their sentences. Joyce got the forty-year federal sentence plus a forty-two-year state sentence for kidnapping and other charges.

WHILE SERVING HER TIME in the federal facility in Pleasanton, California, Joyce met Samantha Dorinda Lopez. Almost a year after Joyce made headlines by forcing a helicopter to land in a prison yard, her California prison confidant, Dorinda, pulled a similar stunt when her escaped-inmate boyfriend, Ron, airlifted her from the prison yard.

Ron and Dorinda managed to add some twists to their helicopter escapade.

The federal prison in Pleasanton was Club Fed before that term became popular slang for a plush prison. The aptly named Pleasanton was part of a nationwide experiment in coed prisons, featuring all manner of amenities, from private rooms to racquetball. According to a 2020 *Esquire* interview with Joyce's friend Dorinda, "If you were gonna be in prison in the eighties, Pleasanton was the place to be."

Was Dorinda a first-class con artist who duped a man with just a few months left on his sentence into helping her escape? Or was she a woman blindly in love who'd been promised protection and riches by a big, successful white-collar criminal? Did Joyce Mattox inspire their romantic helicopter escape by providing details about what to avoid?

When questioned at her trial, Dorinda said she knew Joyce. "She used to hold court and show off her press clippings." Joyce denied providing any assistance.

Ron and Dorinda had fallen in love inside the coed prison before Ron was transferred to a prerelease facility. Despite debate about who came up with the idea, Ron, a decorated Vietnam vet, was the one who brushed up on his flying skills, got a helicopter and flew to Dorinda's rescue. The two were captured when they went to pick up the platinum wedding rings Ron insisted they get. Unfortunately, he paid for them using the same alias he'd used for his refresher flying lessons. Police were waiting at the jewelry store.

Years later, wheelchair-bound in an assisted living facility where she moved after her compassionate release, Dorinda said, "Being with Ron was the best ten days of my life."

In 1989, the South Carolina escape drew another flurry of attention thanks to the CBS movie *The Outside Woman*. Reviews from those who lived the story were mixed. Joyce, then in the federal prison in Marianna, Florida, said she enjoyed watching the TV movie. She said the script changed how she met Smith, and the chase scene was more dramatic than real life, but she "thought it was great."

Members of her family, though, said they wouldn't watch it—they were tired of hearing about the whole affair. James Leonard, the youngest of the escapees, watched it from Kirkland Correctional in Columbia and was less than pleased. "I thought it was sorry," he said. "They had Smith and Ballew blowed up to be some kind of hero and made me look like a fool. It's time for somebody to tell the truth about how it really happened." He said Joyce wasn't an innocent manipulated into the daring escape. Leonard's wife, who had married him in prison a couple of weeks after they met, said if the truth was told, Joyce would never get any reduction in her sentence.

Joyce and Jesse (she called him Glenn) never again got to hold hands or kiss goodbye in a prison visitation room. Jesse Glenn Smith died in September 2002 at age fifty-three in Palmetto Richland Hospital in Columbia. While serving his time at McCormick Correctional Institution, he had been denied parole but would have been eligible for another review in two years. Joyce was released in 2004.

Chapter 4

NEW COLD CASE TECHNOLOGY

The murder of a vibrant "firecracker" of a woman just beginning her life is a tragedy, compounded if the killer isn't caught quickly. Painful questions haunt the family: Did she know him? Do *we* know him? Is he someone we see regularly, someone hiding in plain sight? Are others in danger? The wondering doesn't stop as hopelessness sets in with the grief.

The family of twenty-eight-year-old Genevieve Zitricki couldn't know that her death in Greenville was the start of a series of brutal attacks and deaths that would range over half the country and cover much of the coming decade—or that they'd lack answers for almost two decades.

In April 1990, a coworker of Jenny, as she was known, asked her apartment manager for a wellness check when she didn't come to work. They discovered Jenny dead in her apartment off Villa Road. Investigators found a scene where a killer had taken his time and understood the risks of leaving trace evidence. He had moved her body from the bedroom and left it submerged in the bathtub, with the water running, flooding the bathroom. Her purse and its contents had been dumped in the kitchen sink, also full of water.

Sexual assault, not robbery, was the motive. A warning not to mess "with my family" was scrawled on a mirror. Was that an attempt to distract? Or a clue? Investigators couldn't know at first.

The investigation took the usual path—friends, acquaintances, neighbors and Jenny's ex-husband, who still lived in the apartment complex. Jenny's apartment, where she lived alone following her recent divorce, was near the pool area. All knew her as a gregarious young woman.

The case shocked the community, but leads died out for investigators, leaving her family and friends without answers.

More than nine years later, no one in Greenville and no one in Jenny's family could have an inkling that a murder in Missouri had any connection to Jenny's death. No one would see the connection for almost twenty years, until 2006, when a DNA hit in the FBI's database linked Jenny's death with the 1998 assault and murder of a Missouri mother and daughter. Unfortunately, as in Jenny's case, the Missouri crime had DNA but no name. The murders brought sad news about new victims but no resolution.

Advances in the use of technology in other cases would eventually help the Greenville case. The FBI's CODIS (Combined DNA Index System), introduced in 1998, originally sought to link offenders' DNA with any other offenses they committed across the country. In May 2007, in what became known as the "Grim Sleeper" murders in Los Angeles, CODIS connected a recent death with an alarming eleven unsolved cases dating from 1985. But, as in Jenny Zitricki's case, California's Grim Sleeper still had no name—only the results of his crimes and the DNA he left behind.

However, the Grim Sleeper case became a landmark new use for CODIS. Technology had progressed, and now investigators could search for profiles with sufficiently similar DNA to show a family relationship. Though they didn't have a direct match, they found a close relative of the Grim Sleeper— his son had been arrested on a weapons charge.

To confirm the match, police arranged to work as waitstaff at a restaurant birthday party that the father and suspected killer, Lonnie David Franklin Jr., attended. A test on a pizza crust he left on his plate linked his DNA to ten murders and one attempted murder. This case opened new avenues for investigators around the country.

In August 2018, familial DNA made another crime-solving leap, thanks to genetic genealogy. The arrest of California's Golden State Killer for a series of rapes and homicides spanning two decades from the 1970s introduced cold case squads around the country to a new investigative tool.

While most people use genealogy research websites such as 23andMe.com to search for ancestors, lost family members or perhaps unknown parents, police could now use them to look for murderers. In a growing number of criminal cases, genealogists use birth and death records, obituaries, censuses, property deeds and other documents to piece together family trees related to unknown DNA found at a crime scene.

In Greenville County, a group of retired police investigators who'd volunteered to work the county's cold cases submitted DNA from the Zitricki

FBI ViCAP Alert for the suspected killer of Jenny Zitricki and the Scherers in Missouri. *Released by the FBI.*

scene to Parabon NanoLabs in Virginia, so one of the lab's genetic genealogists could compare that profile with others in a public genealogy database.

Since Parabon began this work in May 2018, the number of solved cases has continued to grow, as has the age of the cold cases solved. Twenty, thirty, forty years later, a killer can be identified, if physical evidence from the scene was properly preserved, if the material hasn't deteriorated and if a perpetrator's relative has uploaded DNA to a database accessible to investigators.

The name Robert Eugene Brashers had never appeared in the Zitricki investigation. Brashers's DNA had already connected him with other homicides and assaults starting in Port St. Lucie, Florida, in 1985—less than five years before Jenny's death. His crimes escalated in brutality and grew more frequent. His range expanded, too, from Cobb County, Georgia, to Tennessee, to Missouri. He'd served time but never for very long.

In January 1999, at a Super 8 motel in Kennett, Missouri, police approached Brashers about a stolen license plate. They had no idea about his alleged crimes. In a standoff, he took his wife, daughter and two stepdaughters hostage before hiding under the bed and shooting himself. He died six days later, on January 19, 1999.

Jenny Zitricki lived for twenty-eight years. It took another twenty-eight years to solve her murder. In October 2018, the Greenville Police Department held a press conference to announce they'd found her killer, thanks to the genetic genealogy match.

Brashers had been dead for almost two decades. At the news conference, Jenny's brother spoke on the family's behalf, commending investigators for not giving up: "Twenty. Eight. Years. It's been a long time," he said.

A long time coming is better than never knowing, but it can't bring back an energetic, much-loved sister or daughter or friend.

As the families of victims were getting some answers to their questions, Brashers's daughter faced questions of her own. Deborah Brashers-Claunch was seven years old when she and her family were hustled out of that motel room in Kennett, Missouri, before her father shot himself. She told *Greenville News* reporter Daniel Gross that Brashers was "an amazing father, a father anybody would have wanted to have." But she also recalled her father's struggles with alcoholism, how he lost control with his daughters and hurt them. He sometimes got in fights or injured himself, just to see if he could take the pain. He would also behave oddly when he came home from one of his extended trips working construction jobs in South Carolina or elsewhere in the Southeast.

As often happens, those exposed to violence inside the home can mistakenly assume that's the norm for everyone. As a child, Deborah had no reason to suspect her father of anything more sinister than losing his temper when he was drunk. But when Greenville police first came to her, asking for a DNA swab to confirm the genetic genealogy match, she "felt in her gut that her father was guilty." She knew he'd traveled for work to the places where the crimes occurred.

When she discovered her father was a serial killer and rapist, Deborah was about the same age Jenny Zitricki was when she lost her life.

Deborah spoke candidly about the damage her father caused. "If I was in front of them and actually talking to every one of the victims he ever hurt, or their families, I'd tell them I was sorry my father was the way he was," she said. "It just makes me sick to my stomach. There's no telling how many lives he ruined."

The timeline of Brashers's known attacks, from 1985 to 1998, raises questions about the blank spaces. He was in a Georgia prison on a gun charge from 1992 to 1997, but where was he and what was he doing during the other gaps when no crimes have been linked to him? Why did his activity escalate in March 1997? Did he commit other crimes where the DNA material can no longer be tested or where matches haven't been attempted? Brashers took the answers to his grave, but his daughter says she wouldn't be surprised if he left more victims. Can new technology solve those crimes?

Chapter 5

TWO LITTLE BOYS

Only a few crime stories stay in the public memory, and even fewer can be brought to mind with only a name or a couple of words, but lots of people in South Carolina and beyond remember Susan Smith.

The story first appeared on the news as a carjacking. A carjacking in a small town like Union, South Carolina, population 9,800? Impossible. And that made it terrifying.

On an October-dark evening in 1994, Susan Smith stopped at a traffic light. A Black man approached, forced her from behind the wheel and drove off with her two boys still strapped in their car seats. The young mother raced to call the police, crying for help to find her babies. Alex, age three, and Michael, fourteen months, had been snatched.

The smooth-faced young secretary with a head of wild blonde hair and her slender grocery-clerk husband, David, appeared on newscasts nationwide. Later, when the real story came out and Susan's news appearances were endlessly replayed and dissected, many viewers could see what had first caused police investigators to question the story they were being told.

For nine days, the search for the boys operated on two separate tracks. One track assumed Susan's account was true. Even before the sun came up the day after her children disappeared, she worked with the South Carolina Law Enforcement Division (SLED) on a composite sketch. It was quickly released to the public and was about as hard to link to a viable suspect as most such sketches are.

John D. Long Lake, east of Union, where Susan Smith's car was discovered nine days after an alleged carjacking. *Photo by Cathy Pickens.*

On the other track, the agents who worked with Susan began noting irregularities. For one thing, witnesses rarely remember more details as time goes on. The story rarely gets more vivid. The story rarely changes at all.

But Susan's did. Not only was the carjacking unbelievable, given the quiet streets on a late October night in a town like Union, but her story simply wasn't holding together. She wasn't acting like other witnesses the agents had interviewed in their long years in law enforcement. She wouldn't look her questioners in the eye. She didn't seem to understand or appreciate the level of expertise and experience they brought to finding her children.

The law enforcement officers talked mostly among themselves about their doubts—until nine days later. On November 3, Sheriff Howard Wells stepped up to the microphones at a news conference.

Susan Smith had confessed.

For nine days, she had lied—to officers, to her husband, to her family, to the national media. Her boys weren't missing. They were strapped in their car seats in her burgundy Mazda Protegé at the bottom of John D. Long Lake, a fishing pond ten miles east of Union off the road toward Lockhart.

Leading up to the sheriff's press conference, the media attention showed only a hint of what would descend on Union during the eight months between Susan's confession and her trial. Reporters set about unearthing the details, trying to make sense of the inconceivable and tragic story of a mother who admitted to killing her own children. They learned the story of Susan Vaughn Smith's life: She worked in the office at a local mill. Her parents divorced when she was young. Her mother had married Beverly Russell, a hometown businessman who was also a state Republican Party committee member and a leader in the Christian Coalition.

After high school, Susan married David Smith, and they had two sons, Alex and Michael, but the marriage was rocky, and the two separated. Both had affairs.

Then reporters pulled out the story behind the veneer. Susan's father, who had adored her, committed suicide just months after her mother remarried. Susan's stepfather sexually molested her, starting when she was about age fifteen. She told her mother and reported the abuse. After some intervention by the authorities, Bev Russell was allowed to move back in with the family. Susan had affairs with the wealthy owner of the mill where she worked and with his son. She struggled with depression and attempted suicide with pills more than once.

The sordid litany filled the tabloid headlines for months.

In July 1995, when Susan Smith's trial began, the street outside the historic courthouse was lined with white party tents on stilts. Under each tent, a TV crew provided a live broadcast. Cameramen and reporters trolled through the crowds that queued up every day, dripping wet in the humid, 110-degree heat index and hoping to get seats inside the courtroom.

In the parking lot to the right of the courthouse, the unmarked car carrying the defendant pulled up close to the steps leading to the side entrance. Cameras weren't allowed inside the courtroom, so photographers lined the fence, scrambling for a shot for that day's newscast. Usually they could grab a few seconds showing her exiting the car and being escorted up the steps in her conservative dress, her head bowed.

The broad front steps of the courthouse led past soaring columns. Inside, the courtroom's dark wooden pews and the subdued light filtering through the windows gave the sense of a somber church service. Seats toward the front were reserved for the press. Everyone else rushed to find a place, knowing they'd have to sit tight without bathroom breaks if they didn't want to lose their spot.

Side entrance to Union County Courthouse, where Smith arrived each morning of her trial. *Photo by Cathy Pickens.*

Front steps of Union County Courthouse. *Photo by Cathy Pickens.*

Before lining up for admittance or as a consolation if they didn't make it inside, some out-of-towners sought out the places around Union that had become so familiar from news reports over the last few months: the graves of Alex and Michael, the house where the young family had lived, the mill owner's mansion on Highway 49 heading west and the boat ramp on John D. Long Lake, off Highway 49 heading east. Crime tourists want to see the locations firsthand, just like history buffs want to see the Liberty Bell or where the D-Day invasion took place. In such a small town, the closeness and ordinariness of it all was the most remarkable feature.

Those who visited the lake to pay their respects, to try to understand what had happened or just to gawk found it remarkably small. How could a pond hide an SUV from view for nine days? The drive from the main road passes through forested land, quiet and serene. At the time of the trial, a memorial to the brothers sat beside the boat ramp, with tributes of flowers or teddy bears or balloons as youthful notes of remembrance.

The boat ramp no longer exists. In 1996, another tragedy struck. A family of five and two family friends parked at the top of the ramp to pay their respects. Something went wrong, and their SUV rolled into the lake, killing all seven. After that, the memorial was tucked under the trees beside the rough asphalt road, before the lake comes into view, and the ramp was removed.

TRIAL WATCHERS HAVE THEIR own motives for coming in person or for poring over the newspaper reports or the television coverage. In this case, the national reporting of the trial showed little sympathy for Susan Smith. The reporting held a bloodlust for justice commensurate with the crime. But over the months, as the dark and complicated story of what went on in the tidy brick ranch houses on the trim, neat streets in Union became tabloid fodder, some reflected that perhaps others were also responsible for what happened to Alex and Michael—those who failed to support Susan after her father's suicide or protect her from the predation of her stepfather. But the young, foolishly romantic woman was the one who climbed the steps to the courthouse every day, waiting to hear if she would live or die.

Tommy Pope, solicitor for York and Union Counties, made the decision to seek the death penalty. Though it wasn't revealed until after the trial, Susan had been willing to plead guilty and be sentenced to life in prison, which in South Carolina at the time would have given her the possibility of parole in thirty years. But Pope felt the case needed to be heard in open court, and Susan's ex-husband, David, pushed for her execution. Community sentiment was high.

Defending Susan were David Bruck and Judy Clarke, who took leave from her job as chief public defense attorney in Spokane, Washington, to work on this case. Clark would go on to represent Unabomber Ted Kaczynski, Olympic Park bomber Eric Rudolph and Boston Marathon bomber Dzhokhar Tsarnaev. Bruck had his own noteworthy trial record in South Carolina. Donnie Myers, the Lexington County, South Carolina solicitor who obtained twenty death sentences, knew Bruck from other cases and called him "an extremely formidable opponent." Both Clarke and Bruck were ardent opponents of the death penalty.

Trial testimony started on Tuesday, July 18, 1995, almost nine months after the boys were killed.

The trial testimony cleared up some of the more shocking assertions made in the tabloids. For instance, one report said Susan stood on the roughened-concrete boat ramp watching her boys struggle in the back seat as the car sank. A heartrending image like that is hard to forget—but it didn't happen.

Union County Courthouse. *Photo by Cathy Pickens.*

In late October, at nine o'clock at night, she couldn't have seen inside the car. That someone's cruel imagination would paint such a picture said more about how listeners were affected by the case than it did about what really happened.

In their testimony, state Department of Natural Resources divers described how they managed to locate the car in the murky water. The lake had been searched earlier, but the car had floated farther than the first searchers expected before it sank. To pull out the car, they had to flip it upright while underwater, then ease it onto the ramp and onto the back of a tow trailer for transport.

Later that same evening, the boys, still in their car seats, were placed carefully in the back of a Suburban and driven by two officers to the state medical examiner in Charleston. A defense objection prevented the officers from testifying about how the events of that night affected them emotionally. Susan, who never took the stand, sat beside her lawyer listening to the testimony and seeing the photos, visibly shaking at times.

A subtle and unexpected element at the trial was the lack of animosity the investigators showed toward the defendant. When questioned on the stand, Pete Logan, the SLED agent who had guided her toward her confession, said her remorse was the "greatest I've seen in thirty-five years."

Susan's brother shared a letter he'd written to her, about how much their dad loved her and about what it had been like for him, at age fifteen, as he banged on the door, powerless to stop his dad from killing himself.

Dr. Arlene Andrews, a professor of social work at the University of South Carolina, provided a counterpoint to the slow drawl and the raw emotion of the witnesses from Union. In evaluating Susan's situation from a clinical perspective, she had found that the people she interviewed always talked about how sweet Susan was, how much she loved her boys. She made friends easily and, in some ways, had a very normal life. But Dr. Andrews also found her emotionally immature, not very resilient, dependent, afraid of being hurt and lacking in meaningful emotional support. Dr. Andrews's summary in court: "Part of her is very damaged."

With most criminal trials, the facts reported in the daily news come in bits and pieces, lack coherence and are hard to fit into a straightforward narrative. With its choppy question-and-answer format and parade of witnesses telling different parts of the story, trial testimony can be hard to follow, to piece together. At this trial, though, after the intense media coverage, each side presented the case in clockwork fashion. Unlike the eleven-month-long O.J. Simpson trial underway in California at the same time, this was no months-long trial; there was no grandstanding for courtroom cameras. This court convened six days a week. The state finished its case on the third day. The entire trial, from jury selection to sentencing, lasted less than three weeks.

ONLY AS THE FULL story was later revealed in books and television documentaries did the intense dual-track investigative work become clear. At the start, Sheriff Wells knew he couldn't waste time protecting his turf. If the boys had been kidnapped, flight across the North Carolina state line, less than fifty miles away, was a distinct risk, so he called in the FBI, along with SLED, to help with the investigation. Those agencies brought tools to the search that Union County couldn't offer.

The suspicions that started that first night, when Susan met with the sketch artist, continued to grow when she seemed too concerned about her appearance before she and David made pleas before the TV cameras for their children's safe return. But the investigators kept talking to Susan. She was their only eyewitness to what had happened—and also a viable suspect. She willingly answered their questions, up until a state profiler angered her. He asked—rather brusquely, she thought—if she'd killed her children. She flew out of the room in angry tears.

After that, Agent Pete Logan took a different approach with her. Dapper and calm, he was one of SLED's most experienced polygraphers. He knew the secret to a successful examination: make the person feel comfortable, gain her trust, act like he had all the time in the world to hear the story she had to tell.

At their first meeting, he and Susan sat in a classroom at a nearby church, away from the apparatus and claustrophobic confinement of a police interrogation room. She was a regular churchgoer; the setting would be less stressful for her. She and Logan spent a couple of hours just talking. Susan told him about her father's suicide. She never mentioned, in those conversations, the sexual abuse by her stepfather.

Logan didn't hook up his polygraph equipment until their second meeting. He asked the baseline questions common in such exams: name, address, questions that showed how she responded when she was telling the truth. He also asked if she'd killed Alex and Michael.

He didn't share the results with her.

After that interview, Logan drove to the lonely intersection where Susan described being carjacked. He sat studying the traffic flow and realized her story couldn't be true. In their next interview, he told her there had to be another car on the scene that night, that the light wouldn't turn red and stop her car unless another car was there on the cross street. Susan decided it must have been another intersection.

Logan had gently built a rapport with her during their interviews. He knew now was the time to push her, and he knew she'd either break or stop talking completely. This November 3 interview was all or nothing. He calmly outlined for her why her stories about the two locations couldn't be true.

Months later, in a hearing to determine whether her confession would be admissible at trial, Sheriff Wells testified Susan was kneeling on the floor, her head bowed into her arms on the seat of a chair, when he joined Susan and Logan at the church. She was sobbing, Wells said. She put her hands in his and told him, "I'm so embarrassed." She asked him to pray.

Wells told the court that in his prayer, "I said there are heavy burdens on this family and on her and on law enforcement and asked the Lord to lead us through this."

She asked for the sheriff's gun.

"Why would you want that?"

"You don't understand. My children are not all right." She was choking and sobbing.

"It's time," Wells said.

Susan had received a much-publicized "Dear Jane" letter from the mill owner's son, telling her she was a nice girl, a good friend, but they didn't have a future together because she had children. She was devastated. Her mind churned with ways to win him back.

Susan said she planned to kill herself and her children. She described buckling the kids in their car seats to take a drive that night. She described parking on the boat ramp in the pitch black, setting and releasing the parking brake more than once. She said she didn't watch the car sink. She ran away, her hands over her ears.

She ran down the long dark road away from the lake, toward the brick ranch house near the main road.

At trial, Dr. Seymour Halleck, a forensic psychiatrist at UNC–Chapel Hill, said yes, Susan was responsible for her actions, but she was also suicidal. "I can only think when she ran out of the car her self-preservation instinct took over."

Wells's press conference, when he announced Susan's arrest and confession, was a bombshell, surprising the public and confirming what those working the case suspected. The two separate tracks of the investigation finally came together.

Road leading to John D. Long Lake. *Photo by Cathy Pickens.*

With the long-lens perspective of more than two decades, the case still mystifies. Academics have studied it as a commentary on gender politics or on the motives of mothers who kill. But most observers made up their minds in those few months in the mid-1990s as the story unfolded before the glare of the TV news cameras. Had Susan intended to commit suicide—something she'd tried before? Or did she kill her children in hopes of a life with a wealthy man? "That is far from the truth," she wrote to a *State* newspaper journalist years later. That charge is what hurts her the most. Even her ex-husband had said she was a good mother.

Chapter 6

THE LADY KILLERS

Motives for murder are remarkably consistent: money, fear, sex, revenge. But the crime scenes resulting from those motives can feel very different in a rural setting than they do in a city. Imagine how different what unfolded on a country road outside Edgefield would have looked had it happened in Boston or even in Columbia, sixty miles away.

Edgefield is small, chock-full of history: it claims ten South Carolina governors but, in the early twentieth century, had a per capita murder rate almost three times that of New York City.

SUE LOGUE

In 1940, rural areas were climbing out of the Depression more slowly than more urban ones. Some folks owned more than others, and what anybody had, they tended to value. So, when a mule wandered into an Edgefield neighbor's pasture and kicked and killed a calf, the calf's owner was understandably upset.

Davis Timmerman's mule shouldn't have been wandering into Wallace Logue's field. Nobody contested that. Logue demanded twenty dollars for his dead calf, and Timmerman agreed to pay. Then Logue decided he needed double that much. Timmerman said no. Things took a bad turn.

Logue went to Timmerman's store to settle accounts. The store was at the junction of Highway 378 and Highway 430, known as Meeting Street, as it runs into Edgefield's courthouse square ten miles away.

When Timmerman refused to pay forty dollars, Logue picked up an axe handle and attacked Timmerman. Timmerman pulled the gun he kept for protection from the counter drawer and shot Logue, killing him.

According to accounts, Timmerman locked the store with the body inside so he could go to town to tell Sheriff L.H. Harling what happened. The sheriff, the coroner and the solicitor drove with Timmerman back to the store.

Hearing the news, folks expected trouble. According to one source, the sentiment around Edgefield was, "If you cuss one of the Logues, then you've got them all to fight."

In March 1941, Timmerman was tried for shooting Wallace Logue, but the jury acquitted him, finding he was rightfully defending himself inside his store.

Having one of their own shot down while trying to collect on a debt didn't sit well with the Logues, especially not with Logue's tiny, dark-haired widow, Sue Stidham Logue. But trouble had been simmering between them

Store where owner Davis Timmerman shot Wallace Logue in 1940. *Photo by Andy Hunter.*

and others in the small community for years, especially after Sue's teaching contract wasn't renewed—when Timmerman was one of the school board members.

Immediately after the verdict, the family began laying their plans. Sue and her brother-in-law, George Logue, knew who to talk to. George and Wallace's nephew, Joe Frank Logue, was a Spartanburg police officer and had been with the family while his uncle was lying in state in the parlor of the large two-story farmhouse. He heard Sue pledge "she wouldn't rest easy until Davis Timmerman was dead."

He would surely know someone who could help balance the accounts.

Sue and George offered $500 (worth more than $9,000 today), and Joe Frank enlisted Clarence Bagwell from Spartanburg to exact the eye-for-an-eye, life-for-a-life justice the Logue clan demanded.

The Logues were willing to wait. No need to draw too straight a line between their ire over Timmerman's acquittal and his death. On September 17, 1941, a year after Wallace died, Bagwell pulled up to the store in a borrowed car. Joe Frank, who'd grown up in the area and didn't want to be recognized, hunkered down in the rear floorboard under a raincoat. He waited while Bagwell went in and emptied a .38 revolver into Timmerman, killing him.

Mrs. Timmerman was working in the yard at their house across the road; she heard the shots, saw the man run from the store. She knew it wasn't any of the Logues; she would recognize them. She raced across the road and found her husband mortally wounded.

Timmerman's death might have become an unsolved tragedy, except that Clarence Bagwell was bad to drink. Within a few weeks, Bagwell spilled the story to a woman who ran a roadhouse he frequented—the Green Gables, which sat near Interstate 585 and Highway 176. Maybe he told the story to Ma Smith to impress her; maybe he talked in his sleep. Either way, she told the sheriff how Bagwell bragged about killing a man in Edgefield and how he now had a pocket full of money.

All four—Clarence the hitman, Joe Frank the police officer, Sue the widow and George the brother—were arrested.

Because the Timmermans and the Logues had deep ties in Edgefield, the judge granted a defense motion to move the trial to the Lexington County court. Joe Frank objected. He preferred to be tried before a hometown Edgefield jury. The other three went to trial first.

Sue and George had been careful to build alibis for themselves at the time of the murder: Sue was out of town, and George was never out of sight of someone in town. But Clarence Bagwell proved a weak link in their chain.

Logue farm, scene of shootout. The farmhouse sat on the bare land at the top of the pond. *Photo by Andy Hunter.*

Former South Carolina Women's Penitentiary, north of Columbia toward Newberry. *Courtesy of Richland Library, Columbia, South Carolina.*

The maxim "No honor among thieves"—or murderers—proved truer than the one about blood being thicker than water. The joint trial began on January 21, 1942. Clarence Bagwell didn't testify against Sue or George, but under unrelenting questioning after his arrest, he had confessed to everything, clearly implicating them. Joe Frank, set to be tried later in Edgefield, took the stand in Lexington and told all about George and Sue soliciting him to find someone to kill Timmerman; about multiple trips between Edgefield and Spartanburg; about Sue handing over a $500 payment—the same amount officers knew Sue had borrowed from the local bank.

The court noted that Joe Frank knew his testimony against Sue, George and Clarence might send him to the electric chair. No prosecutor had offered him a deal; Joe Frank just "wanted to tell the truth 'just as it was, from beginning to end.'" He hadn't received "even sympathy by any official," he said.

The judge didn't allow evidence that would have bolstered Joe Frank's credibility—that he had once been named best police officer in the city of Spartanburg. The jury was allowed, though, to hear how Sue and George Logue had hounded him and finally threatened him into helping them.

The jury deliberated only two hours. Evidence about how Sue and George instigated Timmerman's murder, along with Bagwell's confession of his role, earned them all a conviction for capital murder. All three were sentenced to death in the electric chair.

A year after the trial, on January 15, 1943, in an oddly chivalrous gesture, Sue Logue was the first escorted to the death chamber. Within fifteen minutes, George Logue and Clarence Bagwell followed her.

Six months later, on July 12, Joe Frank Logue's trial in Edgefield started. His testimony had been key to bringing the others to justice, but he, too, was convicted. His execution was set for August 25. His appeal denied, Joe Frank Logue was making final preparations on the day of his execution when Governor Olin Johnston walked into the death house to commute his sentence.

The case might have disappeared into the mass of senseless killings in the state's crime history except for the stories around its edges. For one, Sue Logue had been a primary school teacher at the four-room Tompkins School, even though her appointment caused protests of nepotism. She also, according to gossip, had a particularly close friend in the superintendent of education: Strom Thurmond. Before he was a judge, the governor and one of the longest-serving U.S. senators, Strom, as he is monymously known, had been a teacher.

Joe Frank Logue chose to be tried in his home county, at the Edgefield County Courthouse. *Photo by Andy Hunter.*

Statue on Edgefield town square of Strom Thurmond, South Carolina statesman and Edgefield native. *Photo by Andy Hunter.*

In November 1941, before officers went to the Logue house to arrest Sue and George, someone tipped George off. He enlisted one of his sharecroppers, Fred Dorn, and they ambushed Sheriff Wad Allen and Deputy Doc Clark—Edgefield County's only two paid lawmen. The sheriff was shot in the head and died. Deputy Clark proved a tough fighter, despite his wounds. Sue reportedly got in a lick at him with a chair, knocking him off the porch. The deputy managed to limp or crawl to the road and flag down help, but he succumbed to his wounds days later.

The Old West–style gun battle prompted the state governor to order patrolmen and deputies from neighboring Saluda County to surround the Logue house, and a standoff ensued. Strom Thurmond, by this time a circuit court judge and the only remaining law enforcement official in the county, heard about the siege as he was leaving church. A 1995 *Spartanburg Herald-Journal* article gave Strom Thurmond's account: "I took off my coat and rolled up my sleeves. I wanted them to see I didn't have a gun." He walked the armed gauntlet, got in at the back door and persuaded Sue it was safer to surrender. "I told her those people outside wanted to lynch anybody who had anything to do with this." He put Sue in the back seat of his car, wedged between the sheriffs of Saluda and McCormick Counties, and drove her to the Women's Penitentiary in Columbia.

Logue family plot in Edgefield's East View Cemetery, with small headstones for husband Wallace (*left*) and Sue (*right*). *Photo by Andy Hunter.*

Headstone for Sue Logue, the first woman to die in South Carolina's electric chair. *Photo by Andy Hunter.*

In the end, the calf kicked by a mule led to the deaths of Wallace Logue, Davis Timmerman, Sheriff Allen, Deputy Clark, Fred Dorn, Sue Logue, George Logue and Clarence Bagwell.

A year after her trial, on January 15, 1943, when Sue was transferred from women's prison to the death house, Strom Thurmond was once again on the scene, giving her a chauffeured escort. The man who worked as a statehouse driver said they were "a-huggin' and a-kissin'," according to an interview he gave years later.

Sue Logue had the distinction of being the first of only two women executed in South Carolina's electric chair.

SANDRA BEASLEY/FRANCES TRUESDALE

Often, in small towns, the stories shared at church gatherings or on front porches or around dinner tables tell more truth than what gets reported in the newspaper or told in a court proceeding. The death of Ron "Little Red"

Beasley of Winnsboro was one of those stories, and it took another death for the suspicions of his family and friends to be proven.

In July 1967, police got a call from Sandra Beasley, Little Red's wife. He'd taken a shot at her with a .22-caliber rifle, then put the gun barrel in his mouth and killed himself.

Tragedies like that happen, in towns of all sizes. Only months before, twenty-nine-year-old Little Red Beasley, a welder by trade, had suffered a massive hemorrhagic stroke, leaving him with limited use of one hand and unable to walk or feed himself. He needed constant care. Sandra felt the stress of caring for him and complained to her mother-in-law about it. That couldn't have been easy for Little Red's mother to hear, but apparently his father, K.C. "Red" Beasley, wasn't surprised. He'd never much liked Sandra, thought she had too much control over his son.

When Sandra told Red she couldn't pay for the funeral, Red knew better—and told her so. He knew about the $10,000 life insurance policy. After that exchange, she managed to pay the $2,000 funeral bill without hitting up the Beasleys for the money.

At that time, South Carolina coroners weren't required to have any medical, law enforcement or death investigation training or experience. Coroners were often mortuary workers but could also be insurance agents or farmers—anyone over the age of twenty-one with a high school education. Later, the state legislature changed the requirements to include relevant experience and completion of a death investigation training program. Coroners continued to maintain records for inquests and make the death determination, but they were required to refer the cases of suspicious death to a medical examiner for autopsy.

In 1967, before the requirements changed, Fairfield County's coroner also worked as a barber. Both because Little Red's family made no request and the facts seemed to point to suicide, the coroner filed a handwritten report: "No inquest demanded. No inquest held. Death caused by self-inflicted wound."

Under the circumstances, the family felt they couldn't demand an inquest. After all, Sandra was the only witness. She'd told her story. She also controlled the Beasleys' access to their eleven-month-old grandson. Losing him after losing their son was too high a price, even for justice.

Maybe it wasn't so much a case of covering up the truth as ignoring it. Things were just simpler that way, no need to stir up something ugly—though that didn't sit well with Red Beasley or with Little Red's friend Herman Young. Young had been a pallbearer at the funeral. He remembered pulling up to Little Red's house after the funeral to find what looked like a party in full swing. "I just sat in the yard and cried like a baby," he later told reporter Kim Curtis.

Sandra—who began going by the name Frances—didn't wait long to leave town. A month after the funeral, she married Jerry Truesdale, and they left Winnsboro for Winston-Salem, North Carolina.

In Winnsboro, life settled into its regular routine—until news came twenty years later that Mrs. Frances Truesdale had just lost another husband. Not to suicide but to murder.

This time, Frances's version of what happened changed too much from one telling to another to suit investigators. She and husband, Jerry, were driving home from Virginia at the end of a vacation break from his long-distance trucking job, headed toward Winston-Salem on Interstate 81. Sandra told Jerry's family he was the victim of a drive-by shooting. But she added more details in the story she told police, saying the couple had pulled into a rest stop when two "deadbeats" asked Jerry for twenty dollars. He refused. When they followed him back to his van, he punched one of them in the mouth and drove off. The men, driving a Ford Granada with the letters "RUD" as part of its New York license tag, chased them down the interstate, forcing them to stop. "I have had enough," Jerry said, getting out to confront them. Frances tried to stop him.

The man Jerry had punched in the mouth was the one who then shot him, she said. The men drove off. She got Jerry back into their van and began frantically looking for a hospital. She drove across the highway median to head the other direction, searching for a hospital directional sign. Finally, she used the CB radio to call for help.

Frances told the passerby who responded to her distress call that she hadn't seen her husband punch the man who shot him. The Good Samaritan later told police he smelled gunpowder inside the van and shared an odd statement that Frances repeated eight or ten times: "I didn't mean to do this."

When police arrived at the roadside, they found Jerry lying between the van seats, a single .22-caliber wound behind his left ear. The forty-one-year-old survived in the hospital for two days.

At the hospital, Frances told her sister-in-law yet another story: the men had forced them to stop, pulled open the van door and shot Jerry as he sat in the driver's seat. This time, she could describe the men, and they had New Jersey tags. To the police, she provided even more details about the men and their car, but authorities found no Ford Granada registered in New York with RUD in the license number.

Fairfield County Sheriff's Office in Winnsboro. *Photo by Cathy Pickens.*

Frances also made the serious mistake of lying to police about the amount of life insurance on her husband—she had $285,000 coming to her, not $25,000. She then explained that Jerry had warned her never to tell anyone about their personal worth. She also told police she was unfamiliar with and afraid of guns—testimony that several witnesses at trial contradicted.

Jerry's family knew the rumor about Frances killing her first husband. Jerry Truesdale's younger sister, Anne Letrick, knew the family was concerned when Jerry married her, but when family members raised their concerns, Jerry got angry. That didn't stop Letrick from keeping a written record of every conversation she had with Frances after Jerry was shot, just in case law enforcement would find it useful.

Frances moved from Winston-Salem after Jerry's funeral and opened a restaurant in Carolina Beach. Two years later, she was charged with Jerry's death.

Fairfield County Courthouse in Winnsboro, where Ron "Little Red" Beasley's murderer was tried twenty-nine years after his death. *Photo by Cathy Pickens.*

Sometimes friends and family have to bide their time. Back in Winnsboro, Little Red's friend Herman Young had done just that. In 1965, two years before Little Red's death, Young was hired as the Winnsboro Police Department's first Black officer. Young had bridged many racial divides in his life—including his friendship with Little Red. He'd returned home to South Carolina in the 1960s, after serving as a New York City police officer. He was·the first Black EMT at the Fairfield hospital.

In 1992, Young became Fairfield County's first Black sheriff—and could now begin his own investigation for Little Red, twenty-five years after his friend died.

That same year, Frances Truesdale had taken the stand at her Virginia trial for her second husband Jerry Truesdale's murder—a risky move for any defendant but especially for one who'd given so many differing accounts of what happened on the roadside four years earlier. She was convicted of second-degree murder and sentenced to twenty years. The appellate court upheld her sentence.

In November 1996, another jury—this one in Fairfield County—agreed with Young's long-held belief that his friend couldn't have physically put the rifle in his mouth and shot himself.

Twenty-nine years after Little Red's murder, the jury convicted Frances and sentenced her to life in prison. Little Red's eighty-year-old dad was glad to finally see his son vindicated.

Under her sentence in Virginia, state law allowed Frances eligibility for parole. Sheriff Young presented himself at every hearing, telling the parole board not to free her. She died in prison in July 2014. Herman Young, age seventy-two, retired as sheriff soon after.

Chapter 7

THE MURDER OF FAYE KING

The apparently prosperous may be struggling for money, and the happiest of couples may be locked in bitter enmity, but those outside have little idea until something cracks open the walls of respectability. Often, the crack is caused by a tragedy. When the tragedy is murder, all the neighbors are invited in for a view.

In 1910, the Wilson family—the parents, seven children and Mr. Wilson's elderly mother—moved from their York County homeplace thirty miles north to Shelby, North Carolina, where Mr. Wilson took the job of county tax collector.

In Shelby, daughter Faye Wilson met Rafe King, the commanding, heavyset son of a prominent Shelby family, and they married in 1927. Faye, at twenty-three, was twelve years his junior. They were both attractive and popular, and the marriage seemed like a good match. The couple moved to Faye's York County hometown and rented a house; Rafe took over management of the Wilsons' farm, and Faye taught two courses in French at Sharon High School. For the next year, the couple settled into their roles in their community, attending the Associated Reformed Presbyterian Church, where Faye sang in the choir.

On a Friday morning, January 25, 1929, Rafe King wasn't feeling well. His wife gave him sleeping pills and a kiss mid-morning, on her way out to get milk from the neighbors and to teach her noon French class.

Sometime after three that afternoon, Rafe called from his porch to a boy in the street and asked him to fetch Dr. C.O. Burruss, who examined Rafe and found everything normal, except that Rafe said he couldn't sleep. Dr. Burruss gave him thirty drops of laudanum, a maximum dose of what was known as "whole opium," used at the time for pain relief and as a sleeping aid.

As the day grew late, still unable to sleep, Rafe went to his neighbor's house. His wife had not returned home after her class, he said, so the neighbors volunteered to go look for her. Because he was too sick to search, Rafe stayed with the neighbor's husband. Despite his laudanum dose, he couldn't keep still and headed for the house of the Reverend C.W. McCully, who took him back home and put him to bed.

The preacher looked around the house to see if Faye had left a note, then called Faye's sister in Charlotte and her parents, who were living in Kings Mountain. No one knew where she might be.

At this point, Rafe shared his concern that his wife might have harmed herself. It would be the first of many stories he would tell about Faye, all of them inconceivable to Faye's family and friends.

Others arrived to help search for Faye, including the pastor at her family's Presbyterian church, the Reverend E.B. Hunter. When the sheriff showed up, Rafe said he'd been too sick all day to keep the fireplace going and stayed in bed in the cold house.

Was something odd about Rafe's demeanor that evening? Or had Reverend Hunter observed something about the man over the year of his marriage to Faye? Or was it just the minister's usual inquisitiveness? Whatever the reason, the minister began noticing some oddities. Reverend Hunter loved a good chaw of tobacco. He spit a stream of juice into the fireplace, and it sizzled. He bent to touch the bricks and found they were warm. He began looking around and saw damp spots on the kitchen floor, as if someone had spot-cleaned recently with plenty of water. That he took note of those things spoke of suspicions he didn't share at the time.

The neighbors kept searching outside, even after it turned dark. Their search yielded a sad result. The next-door neighbor lady noticed the door of the small wooden smokehouse was almost closed, when it usually stood open. Inside, they found Faye's body lying on a heap of walnuts. A bottle of Nomoppin, labeled with a skull and crossbones, lay nearby, just beyond Faye's fingertips.

Newspaper reports later said Nomoppin was used as a household cleaner, but the *Charlotte Observer* and newspapers in seven other states advertised it as a treatment for chicken sorehead, a deadly pox for young chicks. In 1939, the U.S. Department of Agriculture seized bottles of Nomoppin in Tampa, Florida, and found McMillan Drug Company of Columbia, South

Sharon Presbyterian Church, founded in 1796, home church for Faye Wilson King. *Photo by Cathy Pickens.*

Carolina, liable for fraudulently misrepresenting its curative powers. The government found Nomoppin contained arsenous acid—a form of arsenic but apparently no remedy for chicken sorehead.

During a more thorough search of the house, a Lysol bottle also labeled "Poison" was found in the plunder room, a storage room near the back porch. At the time, Lysol was formulated with a type of carbolic acid that had a corrosive effect on tissue.

Despite Rafe's claim that his wife had been threatening to harm herself and the assumption by the first doctors on the scene that she'd poisoned herself, neither Nomoppin nor Lysol killed her. Faye King was strangled to death.

The mystery surrounding Faye's death intensified the news coverage. People close to the case were willing to talk, and newspapers reported what they said in detail, though early information was often inaccurate. In the end, Rafe King was arrested and charged with his young wife's murder.

Rafe tried to distract investigators and those asking questions. To bolster his assertion that Faye killed herself, he now claimed she had a venereal disease when they got married, which had caused her to lose her teaching job in Shelby. That wasn't true. He also told people she was pregnant and couldn't bear the thought of going through childbirth, so she killed herself. That also wasn't true. He then claimed she proposed they both drink poison in a suicide pact. No evidence of that, either. He also told the sheriff a dog had been barking outside all day, which meant someone had been lurking around their house. The sheriff should find that man, Rafe said.

Faye had been struck in the forehead and bled on her dress. She had acid burns on her lips, and she'd been laid neatly in the smokehouse with her skirt only slightly askew on one side and one arm raised above her head.

The attack likely happened inside the kitchen. The damp spots on the floor, which the sharp-eyed minister had noticed, supported that theory.

As Rafe's story became less viable, the curious Reverend Hunter continued his detective work. Searching the Kings' house with York County sheriff Fred Quinn, Hunter found blood on a union suit, a style of men's underwear, tucked in a trunk under some clean clothing. They also found stains in the kitchen, on the doors between the kitchen and the dining room, on the floor leading to the back porch and on the floor in the plunder room outside.

THE CORONER'S INQUEST, DELAYED until Solicitor Glenn could clear his calendar to attend, was held on February 4 in the auditorium of Sharon High School, where Faye taught. Onlookers packed the large space, gathered outside the windows and filled the grounds around the building.

After Rafe testified about being in bed all day and stepped from the witness chair, he walked over to Sheriff Quinn and said he wanted to talk.

After hearing testimony about the blood found in the house, Rafe's story shifted again. Now he was certain Faye wasn't killed where she'd been found. He first believed she'd committed suicide, but now, after hearing the testimony, he didn't believe she could have moved her own body. So somebody else must have done it—maybe whoever the dog had been barking at all day.

Solicitor Glenn joined them outside, and Rafe complained how his family "were not giving him a square deal" and wouldn't let him see the newspaper coverage of the case. The sheriff told him, "They are just trying to make you take care of yourself."

Rafe was a man who desperately wanted people to believe he had nothing to do with his wife's death, and he just couldn't quit talking. Trouble was, he told stories before all the evidence was in, and then he had to change his story to something else that also didn't make sense. Rafe just didn't know when to shut up—or maybe he thought he was smart enough to convince folks to see the truth another way.

His chat in the schoolyard with the prosecutor and the sheriff began to draw a crowd, so the officials led him inside to a classroom where they could talk in private. One of Rafe's brothers eventually found him sequestered in the classroom with the two lawmen and led him away. As the sheriff and solicitor followed them down the hall, they overheard his brother warning him, "You ought not to talk to them. You have talked too damn much already."

The coroner's jury decided Faye died from poison "administered by hands unknown to us."

As soon as the inquest verdict was announced, Glenn issued an arrest warrant for Rafe King, who turned himself in. On February 7, just three days after the inquest, Rafe was released on a $3,000 bond. He went home to Shelby with his parents.

FAYE DIDN'T GET TO rest so easily. Two weeks after her burial, her body was exhumed to answer some of the questions Rafe had raised at the inquest. At the upcoming trial, Dr. Burruss, who performed the first autopsy, would have to admit that was his first and only autopsy. The prosecution knew they needed answers only a second, more detailed exam could provide.

The second postmortem dismissed one of Rafe's claims: Faye was not pregnant.

Even though the body had been injected with embalming fluid, examiners sent the stomach and its contents to a chemist at Clemson College for analysis, even though poison now seemed an unlikely cause. A more detailed examination of the tissues of Faye's throat showed she had been strangled with a heavy cord. The bloody wound on her forehead continued along her scalp, hidden by her hair, and may have been enough to stun her or knock her unconscious before she was strangled.

On the day of Faye's death, Dr. J.H. Saye was one of the first doctors to examine the body. Later, Saye's married daughter, Mrs. Bankhead, gathered with some other women to prepare Faye for burial. Mrs. Bankhead wanted to iron the belt of Faye's kimono but found the electric iron wouldn't work. The cord seemed stretched, so she sent someone to find a stovetop flat iron. After the second autopsy established that a cord was used to strangle Faye, Mrs. Bankhead got word to the sheriff about the malfunctioning iron.

The investigation was far from over. More than two weeks after the inquest, Sheriff Quinn and York police chief Frank Faulkner went to the King house to cut out the bloodstained portions of the kitchen floor and doors. They noticed, in one of the closets, an access hole to the attic. Faulkner had one just like it in his house, he said. Curious, he got a chair and climbed up for a look.

Nothing was stored in the attic, so no one had searched there. When Faulkner's flashlight beam hit the dust at an angle, he saw a trail of disturbed dust along the joists leading to an eave above the front porch. Easing his way past the rafters, he found a bundle of clothing tucked into the framing of the eave. Tied up inside a man's shirt were a coat, a vest and a pair of trousers, all bloodstained, "especially on the front of the coat and on the cuff of one of the sleeves." The tailor-made coat had the initials RFK on the lining. Who else but Rafe F. King? Storing discarded clothes in the far reaches of the little-used attic couldn't have an innocent explanation.

With that discovery, the sheriff, the police chief and the solicitor all headed to Laurens the next morning to petition Judge Watts to rescind King's bail. The judge refused. Rafe King remained free.

These discoveries and other evidence would tie Rafe's haphazard, ever-changing story into a more concise tale for the jury when he came to trial a few months later.

The story of the lovely young teacher and her handsome husband, both from prominent families, captivated the crime-minded and curious in the region. An enterprising man, C.E. McGuckin, signed a lease on the empty Sharon house the Kings had rented. On Sunday, February 24, he opened it for tours, charging a quarter a head. A good thing the investigators had returned to get what evidence they needed before the flood of tourists started. Visitors wanted souvenirs and spirited away doorknobs and chunks of wood.

One oft-told tale of the tourists was that of the "society lady of Clover" who hadn't gotten word about the tour's admission fee and didn't bring any money with her. Mr. McGurkin wasn't about to bend the rules, society lady or no society lady. A chivalrous gentleman from Gastonia loaned her a dollar.

WITH SO MUCH LOCAL interest in the case, Rafe's attorneys asked for a change in venue away from York County to somewhere less prejudicially invested in the case. As expected, the solicitor opposed moving the trial. The defense attorney opposed moving it to Chester because Solicitor Glenn was from there, as was the state's chief medical witness, who happened to

The King trial was moved from York County to the historic Chester County Courthouse. *Photo by Cathy Pickens.*

be Glenn's brother-in-law. The frontrunners in the betting were Fairfield or Lancaster Counties.

The judge ruled that the recently refurbished Chester courthouse would host the trial. The courthouse won appreciative comments from trial-goers and the press when the proceedings convened on July 1, 1929, just over five months after the murder. Reports said the trial was expected to cost Chester County $7,000, the equivalent of more than $100,000 today.

Squared off for battle on each side was a cartload of lawyers, each known in the region for his trial skills. At Rafe King's table sat lead attorney Thomas F. McDow from York, along with a former North Carolina congressman and a judge from Shelby, three attorneys from Chester and another from York.

County solicitor Harry Hines was aided by a former South Carolina senator from Chester, two other attorneys from Chester and three from York. Fourteen attorneys in all were arrayed to do battle over Rafe King, to send him to or save him from the electric chair.

After pretrial arguments about what evidence could be included, Judge Henry Johnson ordered that the clothing Faye wore, the bundle of clothes from the attic, the suit of underclothing, some of Faye's school papers and books, the bottle of Nomoppin and the bloodstained pieces of wood and carpet could be introduced as evidence. Though heavily contested by the defense attorneys, who still hoped to use poisoning to raise reasonable doubt about the cause of death, the Clemson chief chemist's testimony was also allowed.

The trial opened on July 1, 1929, and it commanded banner headlines in the *Charlotte Observer* even after it ended ten days later. The court met through long, hot summer days without a break for Independence Day. Jurors didn't even go to church on Sunday. Instead, they got a Sunday drive to Winnsboro and Great Falls as an outing. Some speculated the three-car entourage might visit the murder house. They didn't.

The crowds vying for seats in the courtroom only grew as the days went by.

Part of the problem with fitting in the spectators was that two sections of seating had to be reserved for the dozens of witnesses who would be called.

Sensational trials are not a recent phenomenon. This one had some elements that would have made headlines if the case occurred one hundred years later and some elements that would now be considered quaint.

The state introduced evidence that Rafe, far from being prosperous, was desperate for money. He tried to get Faye's sister's husband, W.C. Reagan of Charlotte, to give him a $3,000 mortgage against the estate of Faye's mother, so he could repay a $1,000 loan he'd already taken against the estate, with $2,000 in cash left to pay his other debts. Faye's brother-in-law refused. Reagan also testified that Faye once joked that Rafe and his second wife would have a good time on her life insurance money.

The jury heard that $5,000 in life insurance (worth almost $80,000 today), payable to her husband, had been taken out five months and ten days before her death. Another witness said her husband had been in touch with an agent eight or ten days after Faye's death about collecting $1,000 of the insurance.

On another issue, the defense contended that Faye didn't want to have children and was terrified of childbirth and that the bloodstained clothes in the attic had been planted—though they never suggested who had reason to incriminate Rafe King. Rather, Rafe's attorneys said he was always kind and generous to his wife.

After the defense thoroughly dismantled Dr. Burruss for his lack of experience and mistakes in the first autopsy, in which he and Dr. Saye determined Faye died from poisoning, the key witness became B.F. Robertson, chief chemist for toxicological work at Clemson College. Robertson's testimony was detailed and lengthy. The body had been embalmed before the second autopsy, when the stomach and contents were removed, so Robertson described how he compared the stomach contents with the chemicals found in the embalming fluid as well as in the Nomoppin. His crucial conclusion: poison did not cause Faye's death.

The second autopsy also revealed bruising and damage to blood vessels in her neck, most likely caused by a cord. Headlines in the *Observer* summed up the critical testimony of the day: "Faye King Strangled, Doctor Testifies." Later in the week, Dr. R.E. Abell testified in detail about the second autopsy, explaining that the head wound had not fractured the skull or injured the brain and didn't cause Faye's death, that the wound circling the neck was serious enough to cause damage through the skin and muscles, that bruises were observed on the elbows and knees and that some sort of caustic substance was found under her tongue. He explained that if someone swallows liquid, it's unlikely to end up under the tongue, implying that Faye was in no condition to swallow anything when the caustic liquid was poured in her mouth.

On cross-examination, the lawyers went after the doctor, trying to find a weak spot. No, he admitted, he'd never performed an autopsy on a body buried for months, as Mrs. King's had been. And he admitted the broken blood vessels in the neck didn't rule out suicide. The newspaper report left the impression that the defense attorneys fought mightily but won little in that exchange.

IN THE DAYS BEFORE television coverage and sound-byte-sized attention spans, newspapers provided detailed accounts for those who couldn't squeeze into a courtroom. On the trial's third day, the *Charlotte Observer* reported, "Court opened this morning with many more women in the courtroom than was the case on Monday [when the preliminaries, such as jury selection, took place]. Their gayly colored dresses provided an attractive note in the otherwise more or less drab room. King was dressed the same as he was at the opening of the trial, wearing a blue suit, soft white shirt, with a blue bow tie, black shoes and sox. He did not appear to be as fresh as yesterday."

The comment about women brightening the courtroom wasn't echoed by a *Yorkville Enquirer* editorial reprinted in several papers. "Girls and Sex in Court" decried how many high school girls crushed to be in the courtroom, "listening without a blush as the most intimate details of the Kings' sexual relationship were discussed." Some reporters said, "They ought not let those girls in here." But they "entered laughing and chattering loudly." What was revealed openly in court in front of these young girls would have been illegal if printed and sent through the mails, the editor said. But defense lawyer Glenn countered, saying young girls knew more than their elders. According to historian Miles Gardner, the editorial writer noted that "the last redoubt of the oldtime, unsophisticated, refined and sensitive, charming and bashful girls is, or was, in the South and especially South Carolina, but observation for a week in old Chester, South Carolina, seems to prove conclusively that the modern girl has abandoned that redoubt and gone over to her sisters in Illinois, Pennsylvania, California and the Dakotas."

So, what was so shocking about the testimony? Rafe King knew he had a venereal disease when he married Faye, and he passed the infection on to her. He'd suggested that caused her despair and willingness to kill herself—and after her death, he blamed her for the infection.

The newly renovated courtroom got plenty of compliments. Mary Alys Voorhees, in the *Charlotte Observer*, provided color commentary on the trial, giving readers a sense of what went on in the courtroom other than the testimony. Reporters at the press table shared a laugh at the expense of a defense attorney who asked if he could have some ice water from their pitcher: "Sure," said the reporter from the *Yorkville Enquirer*. "It's real news when a lawyer drinks water."

Good trial lawyers are typically good storytellers, and the most-repeated anecdotes came from the lead defense attorney. Thomas F. McDow told the press table that he'd last been in the Chester courtroom "trying a case involving a jackass alleged to have been killed by a rail train. We did not put the dead jackass on the stand but, if I remember correctly, several others testified."

On the final days of the trial, as the lawyers gave closing arguments and the judge instructed the jury on the law they should apply, the crowds outside the courtroom continued to grow. Six lawyers from each side made arguments, spaced over two days.

Judge J.K. Henry had asked a retired minister to open court every day with a prayer. When the jurors retired to consider the case, the group decided they didn't need another prayer before they began deliberations; the case had been prayed over enough to cover it. The twelve set to work reviewing the evidence. The first vote was eight in favor of first-degree murder, four for second degree. On a third vote half an hour later, they were unanimous for first-degree murder.

On Tuesday evening, July 9, a little over a week after the trial began and only two hours after the judge gave them the case, they returned with a guilty verdict.

John Voorhees recorded Rafe King's reaction to the verdict: "King's chin went up in the air a couple of inches like someone had hit him on the jaw. He gazed in the direction of the window with a look of reflection upon his face for a minute, wet his lips with his tongue and then a ghost of a smile that had formed on his face broke into a full-fledged smile and he laughed before he left the room for jail a few minutes later."

On Wednesday, the judge delivered the sentence: death by electrocution. As he was handcuffed, Rafe said, "I am ready to die, and I will die an innocent man."

A quirk in the paperwork meant that Rafe King continued his stay in the Chester County jail for a few more days before he could be moved to death row in Columbia. Though visitors weren't allowed inside the jail, the number of people—even women and children—who came to visit with Rafe from the sidewalk outside his cell annoyed the building's housekeeper, "so she expressed herself."

When the high-profile defendant and plenty of lawyers on both sides finally left town, the streets around the Chester courthouse calmed down, but the case wasn't over. In the inevitable appeal, half of the state supreme court's lengthy opinion was a reprint of Judge Henry's instructions to the jury.

The opinion, published in October 1930, noted that it took a while to appeal the case because the trial transcript was so long: 946 pages, with the defense attorneys making eighty-one exceptions to what went on during the trial. An appellate court isn't permitted to deal with questions of fact; facts are decided by the jury. An appellate court can deal only with issues of law, such as something that may have violated the defendant's right to a fair trial. The appellate court made a thorough analysis of the defense's objections and found enough that merited granting Rafe King a new trial.

Again, Rafe's attorneys wanted to keep the case out of York County. Round two of the drama would play out in the Lancaster County Courthouse, designed—as were at least eighteen of the state's courthouses—by South

Carolina architect Robert Mills, who also designed the Washington Monument. As with the Chester courthouse, Lancaster's then-hundred-year-old courtroom provided too little room for all who wanted to see the trial.

Gathering all the lawyers for another trial delayed the proceedings until May 1931. This time, solicitor W. Gist Finley led the state's team, and lawyers from two Lancaster firms joined Thomas F. McDow. Judge C.C. Featherstone from Greenwood presided.

The Associated Press opened its trial coverage with a journalist's trumpet call: "Out of a maze of legal entanglements, King has emerged from the shadow of the death chair" for his new trial in Lancaster, "which boasts that no white man has ever been sentenced to death in its court."

The judge was determined to avoid the criticism the defense lawyers leveled at the first trial, where an antagonistic crowd was allowed to gather too close to King and "to show its hostility by its demeanor."

On May 4, court convened, the jury was chosen and several witnesses for the prosecution took the stand—all before the lunch break. The trial started with the testimony of the Reverend Ebenezer Hunter, whose stream of wet tobacco juice sizzling in what should have been a cold fireplace helped turn the investigation toward Rafe two years earlier.

Robertson, the Clemson chemist, testified that the portion of stomach wall he examined showed carbolic acid of the kind used in the embalming fluid, with no sign of poison.

In both trials, the state presented an unorthodox but effective demonstration. Dr. W.C. McMillan, the Columbia producer of Nomoppin, testified the amount of poison in the preparation wasn't strong enough to harm a human. He held Nomoppin in his mouth for several seconds before spitting it in a cuspidor. (Some accounts said he drank it.) The liquid left no burns in his mouth.

The testimony in the second trial was remarkably quick. An *Observer* reporter noted the defense attorneys cut off questioning as soon as they got the answers they sought, without digging further. And once again, the defendant did not testify. No lawyer wants to put a talkative and unpredictable defendant on the stand, and Rafe's attorneys feared he might lambast the prosecuting attorney or call all the witnesses against him liars.

A reporter also noted the judge ruled in favor of every defense objection. Judge Featherstone apparently planned to leave no opening for the state supreme court to overrule this decision.

After a week of testimony, the jury returned with a guilty verdict and a recommendation of mercy. The defense attorneys had won what they

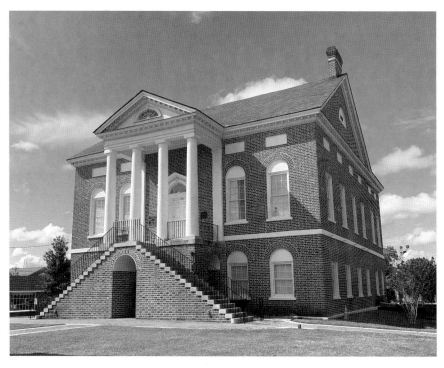

The second trial was moved to the Lancaster County Courthouse, one of many in the state designed by Robert Mills. *Photo by Cathy Pickens.*

came for: Rafe King escaped the death penalty. Those who watched the second trial felt the jury decided on the less severe verdict because it wasn't clear the murder was premeditated. Many felt Rafe King hadn't planned to kill Faye, that an argument had gotten out of hand. If he'd planned it, perhaps his accounts wouldn't have wandered and changed so much. On the other hand, accusing his wife of committing suicide and blaming her for a venereal disease didn't endear him to either of the juries or to the public who followed the case.

Rafe served his sentence at the South Carolina Penitentiary in Columbia and died there of heart disease in 1949.

In December 1931, a few months after the second trial, *True Detective* magazine reported the case. The *Lancaster News* seemed pleased that the retelling wasn't "colored to make the story more interesting" but also noted with apparent regret that the article gave only passing attention to the Lancaster trial.

Chapter 8

THE WITCH TRIALS

S ince 1692, Salem, Massachusetts, has served as both object lesson and tourist attraction for witch hysteria in the United States. Perhaps New England had better publicists than South Carolina? Or perhaps it's best that South Carolina missed out on making headlines for witch trials and that Arthur Miller didn't set his classic Broadway play *The Crucible* in Fairfield County.

But he could have. In 1792, a century after Salem's trials, a witch trial was held in what is now Fairfield County. South Carolina lawyer Philip Edward Pearson included an account in *History of Fairfield County*, a manuscript he wrote before he left for Alabama and Texas in 1838. A biographical sketch published in 1859 said Pearson was "fond of antiquarian researches and preserving legendary lore" and a good lawyer who prepared and argued his cases well but "never very long, which was, then and is now, most commendable."

Pearson personally knew one of the accused witches, and one of his kinfolk—a General Pearson who had holdings and an apple orchard on the Broad River—may have been involved in the goings-on.

Lee R. Gandee, a native son who researched and wrote about the region, told the story of the witches of Fairfield in the January 1970 issue of *Fate* magazine. This witch outbreak is unusual for a couple of reasons: for one, the alleged witches were tried and tortured in a makeshift judicial proceeding held on a plantation outside Winnsboro, but none were killed. The other oddity: one of the convicted witches sued one of her tormentors for monetary damages—and won.

The German settlers in Fairfield County likely migrated from the Saxe-Gotha township south of the Congaree River in current Lexington County and from what later became Dutch Fork—"Dutch" used to describe Germans. South Carolina had robust immigration policies, trying to bring in settlers to provide a buffer between indigenous tribes and the lucrative indigo and rice production that made Charleston the wealthiest city in the colonies.

According to one politician, in an area with too few trained ministers and formal churches, the Germans in Dutch Fork "from a pious desire of having some religion had unhappily formed a Sect of Enthusiasts." Fairfield's German settlers would have known of the scandal of Jacob Weber and his Gifted Brethren followers and the murders Weber committed in 1760.

Anglican missionary Charles Woodmason wrote of the "Diabolical Minds" of Weber's followers as he traveled the Carolina Backcountry trying to convert the Presbyterians and Baptists and "children of the forest." Other ministers added details to the tale, demonstrating that cults are nothing new and that perhaps some modern cults are tame by comparison. The story was too strange to forget.

Jacob Weber and two of his followers—Smith Pieter and a slave named Dauber—declared themselves the tripartite godhead, with Weber as the Father, Smith Pieter as the Son and Dauber as the Holy Ghost. As can happen in attempts to establish Heaven on Earth, the triune had a falling-out. Weber told his followers that Smith Pieter was the old Serpent and must be put to death to save the world. Full of conviction, Weber's followers fell on Smith and beat him to death. For good measure, the sect members also killed Dauber and another man, Michael Hans.

Weber and four of the six defendants were convicted and sentenced to death. Following Weber's execution, the others received reprieves, the community's bloodlust apparently sated.

Extremist religious views and witches weren't unknown among settlers coming from different regions in Europe. Over the years, immigrants brought with them those who used natural medicines or hexes, practices usually seen as beneficial rather than dangerous black magic. But something changed in Fairfield in 1792. Things got ugly, and some citizens organized to stamp out what they saw as a demonic threat.

The role of lead witch belonged to Mary Ingelman, a woman of German descent whom Pearson described as "a remarkably neat, tidy and decent old lady" whose "conversation was pleasant, entertaining, instructive; her manners mild, simple and agreeable." She was known for her ability to use "simples" to cure her neighbors of their complaints.

Though decent, pious, helpful Mary Ingelman was the chief target, charges were also brought against the Hardings, a husband and wife, and Sally Smith, "an old crone." One report described the women as over eighty years of age, though another historian, writing in 1942, gave a slightly different version of Pearson's account: "I can barely remember having seen one of the sisterhood in the hands of the officers of this court, a poor old German woman 70 years of age, going to the place of trial, and afterwards to have seen the scars of the cowskin on her arms and shoulders."

The charges claimed the four accused witches tormented the two Henley sisters, biting them and sticking them with pins and splinters. Such was Mary Ingelman's occult power that not even four men could keep Rosy Henley from levitating off her bed.

A local warlock wasn't brought to trial, even though he too was said to have tormented another duo of sisters, allegedly levitating one off the bed and sliding her across the ceiling and along the wall without harming her. In that case, though, the requisite four strong men managed to prevent further levitations.

Mary Ingelman also allegedly tormented another woman, made her vomit up balls of hair full of pins and deprived her of all peace and comfort by sticking her with pins and splinters.

Mary's son testified against her, saying she broke his cow's neck when she raised it up in the air and dropped it after he refused to give her the cow. Her grandson said she'd turned him into a horse and rode him to General Pearson's orchard. While she was filling her bag with apples, he reached his long horse neck up to grab one, and she punched him hard in the cheek.

Mr. Collins, a neighbor, claimed Mary came to him with her arm in a sling and blamed him for her injury—caused when he shot at a deer that turned into a black cat with a wounded foot. She later turned that neighbor into a horse and "rode him to a convention of witches." When the devil himself commended her on her "splendid horse," she told him, "This is that rascal Collins."

Pearson's account says that, when presented with the evidence, neither Mary nor the others made any attempt to defend themselves. Of course, one wonders how anyone would respond to such accusations, especially after being hauled miles away from home to a shed on the grounds of a strange, grand house to face accusers.

At Thomas Hill's plantation, a "jury" had been selected, and the testimony was heard in an outbuilding. After their "conviction," the four old people were hung by the wrists from ceiling joists and flogged—the newspaper said "brutally." Then they were "placed with their feet to a bark fire and confined there until their soles popped off." The others crawled away, but someone caught Sally Smith on the road and pinned her to the ground with a "pine log across her neck. She could not stir and the next day was relieved by a benevolent person passing along the path."

Unlike Salem's trials a century earlier, no one in Fairfield was hanged. Hard to believe, but none of the octogenarians died from their tortures, either. The witch hunters were apparently considering who else in the community needed to be singled out for their powers or associations with the devil, but a preacher stepped in with an effective counter to the hysteria.

Word around Fairfield that Preacher Woodward would be delivering a sermon on witchcraft drew a large Sunday crowd. Woodward was the son of an old Fairfield family. He'd fought in his father's Revolutionary War militia, involved in most of the major fighting in the Carolinas. Woodward returned home to farm, was ordained as a Baptist minister and later served in the U.S. and state houses of representatives.

Woodward's parishioners were in high dudgeon over the evil circling their community, but despite its exciting premise, his sermon didn't follow the theme many expected.

Preacher Woodward said yes, witches and sorcery and magic are active in our world. But why, he asked, would witches, given their supernatural powers to be whatever they wished, choose to be old and ugly? Wasn't it more likely a witch or a wizard would be young and vital and beautiful? The preacher's tone apparently carried the wry humor he intended, because soon the congregation was laughing along with him. The torments ceased. Lee Gandee wrote in *Fate*, "Witchcraft and laughter cannot coexist."

Periodically, usually around Halloween, newspapers report that Mary Ingelman haunts the courthouse in Winnsboro because of her mistreatment—never mind that her witch trial didn't happen at the county courthouse but in an outbuilding on Thomas Hill's farm. She did, though, come to the courthouse—one older than the current 1823 courthouse— to bring her lawsuit against John Crossland. He was probably a tenant farmer of Hill's and was appointed "sheriff" and "executioner" in the bogus proceedings.

Mary swore out the warrant before the Reverend William Yongue, a Presbyterian minister willing to stand up to public sentiment against Mary. Crossland was ordered to pay a judgment of ten pounds sterling and court costs, but he took off for the "far west," which, according to Pearson, would have been Georgia or Alabama at the time. None of the wealthier or more prominent of Mary's accusers were ever brought to trial. So perhaps she is indeed waiting around the courthouse, looking for justice.

THOUGH MARY INGELMAN IS the only accused witch to seek judicial recompense, she wasn't the last South Carolina witch brought before a public tribunal. Around 1813, some twenty years after the Ingelman case, a Lancaster girl accused Barbara Powers, an elderly Fairfield resident, of sitting on her, choking her, turning her into a horse and riding her to Cheraw, a distance of roughly fifty miles. According to the girl, Powers slipped through keyholes to steal from shops in Lancaster, then loaded up the horse—that is, the girl-turned-horse—to carry the goods to Chesterfield and on to Cheraw.

The girl told Judge David Johnson that "her health and strength declined from the severity of the almost incessant hardships in the service of the witch." His curiosity piqued, the judge asked her to give testimony under oath. After she told of her suffering, the judge halted the proceedings. He sent some folks to Chesterfield to get Powers and bring her to Lancaster to heal the girl. Barbara Powers reportedly touched her and pronounced "God bless you" over her, and the girl "instantly recovered."

Suspicions of witchcraft could grow from misunderstanding or from meanness—or ignorance. According to some historians, Swiss-Germans like Mary Ingelman may have practiced a laying-on-of-hands faith healing which appeared supernatural to their Scots-Irish neighbors. Or their accents and folkways may have marked them as "other."

Pearson's account is the best-written record we now have. Mary Ingelman's successful lawsuit, the community's shock over the vigilante trial at the Hill Plantation and Preacher Woodward's satiric sermon ended the worst of the witch scares in the South Carolina backcountry. In Powers's case, Judge Johnson's healing ceremony continued to demonstrate the power of humor and kindness over suspicion and fear.

Chapter 9

THE HIGHWAY 93 MURDERS

C lemson sits on Lake Hartwell in the foothills of the Blue Ridge Mountains, more rural and small-town than the state's other large universities. The university's twenty thousand students come from across South Carolina and the world to enroll in engineering, agricultural, business and technical studies. But some students choose Clemson for its proximity to water sports and fishing on Lake Hartwell and to the mountains for hiking, camping and river rafting.

A small-town atmosphere and plenty of outdoor activities would seem ideal for parents wanting to send a child off to a safe, wholesome college. But image isn't always reality.

NORSAADAH HUSAIN'S UNSOLVED CASE

On June 16, 1992, the janitor at the Suds and Duds Laundromat on Highway 93 in Central came on duty at 8:42 p.m. A car was parked out front, but no one was inside on that Tuesday evening. As soon as he saw blood on the floor and a long, red streak, as though something was dragged from the dryer area to the front door, he called the Central police.

The hood of Norsaadah Husain's white Datsun felt warm to the touch, so it hadn't been parked long enough to cool off. A load of clothes was in a dryer, and her car keys were on top of a washing machine. Police found a

View of Highway 93, downtown Central. *Photo by Jack Grooms.*

bloody handprint on a metal support post. Whatever had happened inside the laundry that evening, Norsaadah fought hard.

Norsaadah was a thirty-year-old graduate student from Ranwang, Malaysia, enrolled in Clemson's food science program. Her particular interest was tea, and in an Anderson *Independent-Mail* interview, one of her professors recalled a trip they'd taken to the Charleston Tea Plantation (now Charleston Tea Garden) on Wadmalaw Island. She hoped to use her education to benefit the tea industry in her home country.

Dozens of officers in a multi-district task force drawn from Central police, Clemson police, Clemson University police, the Pickens County Sheriff's Office and the South Carolina Law Enforcement Division (SLED) searched for Norsaadah. But as the investigation continued into a third month, hope wore thin.

That September, after deer season opened, a hunter in the woods outside Salem, in Oconee County, came across skeletal remains covered in leaf debris near Duke Power's Oconee Nuclear Station. The clothing Norsaadah was wearing the day she disappeared was piled next to the bones.

The autopsy found a nick or groove cut into one of her vertebrae, indicating she may have been stabbed in the neck. Rips in the discarded clothes suggested stab wounds and perhaps a sexual assault, but neither the body nor the scene revealed much other information.

Investigators weren't ignoring the ominous similarities with another abduction and still-unsolved murder. Four years earlier, in 1988, another victim's body had been dumped not far from where Norsaadah was found. Daisy Ruth Snider, forty-two, disappeared after attending church at Geer Memorial Baptist in Easley on November 27. The church was easily visible from Highway 93 and about fourteen miles from the laundromat in Central. Daisy Ruth's car was found, with her groceries still inside, parked near the walking track at Easley Junior High School. A few days later, her body was found not far from the Duke Power nuclear reactor site. She'd been strangled and shot.

Sixteen years later, in 2004, the Snider murder was solved with the help of DNA collected at the time of her death. Mark Neal Golden was already serving a sentence for homicide in Pennsylvania. He pled guilty and will be transferred to South Carolina should he ever be released in Pennsylvania.

Despite the proximity of the kidnapping and dump sites, the cases appeared to be unrelated, and the Snider case offered no help in solving Norsaadah's murder.

In 1992, Norsaadah's two brothers flew to the United States to claim her remains and return her to Malaysia. Decades after they sent their daughter and sister far from home to pursue her dreams, her family still has not gotten any answers to what happened that night at the laundromat. In 2013, when the Oconee Sheriff's Office posted its cold cases on a new website, Norsaadah's story was included, with a request for any leads.

BROOKE HOLSONBACK'S UNSOLVED CASE

About nine thirty on the evening of February 19, 1997, Brooke Holsonback stopped by the dorm room of her Clemson classmate Bryant Gallup. He and his friend Jeff Dubnansky had decided to go mud-bogging in a four-wheel-drive Jeep and invited her to go along. The two had been drinking, so Brooke agreed to drive them to the site.

Eighteen-year-old Brooke had moved from tiny Prosperity, South Carolina, northwest of Columbia, for her freshman year in Clemson's biochemistry program. At Saluda High School, she had been an outgoing cheerleader and a good student. The oldest of three siblings, she'd always known she'd be a Clemson Tiger when it came time for college.

Brooke drove the Jeep a few miles from campus, toward Seneca, where Bryant and Jeff could drive the four-wheel-drive vehicle off road. At some point, the Jeep ended up mired in the mud, and the two guys started arguing, then had a physical tussle about who was at fault. They said Brooke was sitting on the tailgate while they worked it out, but when they looked up from their scuffle, she was gone.

The campus was only about three miles away. But would Brooke have taken off on her own on a cold February night, walking along dark roads back to her dorm room?

Gallup and Dubnansky said that's what must have happened. After their fight, they looked for Brooke, then figured she'd walked to campus. Bryant waited with the marooned Jeep while Jeff left on foot to find help.

About noon the next day, Brooke's roommate contacted university police to report that she hadn't returned to their room in Johnstone, the old dorm students called the Tin Cans.

Police didn't have to mount a search. About the time Brooke's roommate reported her missing, a construction worker called. He was taking his lunch break at a picnic table overlooking Lake Hartwell when he saw a body floating near the boat ramp off Highway 93, across from what locals knew as the YMCA or Y beach.

Brooke Holsonback's death was due to strangulation and drowning; she may have been sexually assaulted, but the evidence wasn't clear.

Three decades earlier, in 1966, disgruntled Clemson citizens had seceded from Oconee County. In an annexation vote, the town of Clemson became part of Pickens County, along with the university and about 1,600 residents. In 1997, Lake Hartwell divided the two counties, so Clemson sat in Pickens County, while the lakeside area where Brooke was found sat in Oconee County. The Oconee Sheriff's Office took the lead in the investigation, working with the Clemson University Police Department and SLED.

Investigators first talked to Bryant and Jeff, the two students who last saw Brooke. Despite intense interest in the case, no suspects were named, and no formal charges were made in the months that followed.

Over the years, periodic reports on the case appeared in the news. On the twentieth anniversary in 2017, a task force announced a fresh look, using

The view across Lake Hartwell and Highway 93 bridge toward campus, the football stadium and Tillman Hall clock tower. *Photo by Jack Grooms.*

new profiling techniques. At that time, Captain Greg Reed with the Oconee Sheriff's Office told *True Crime Daily* that physical evidence was scant. Rain and mud destroyed anything they might have found in the area where the trio went four-wheeling. Being submerged in the lake washed evidence from Brooke's body. Captain Reed said the polygraph exams both men took showed signs of deception, though the results aren't admissible in court. He felt they had enough evidence to prosecute a case, but the county solicitor didn't agree.

With that 2017 news report, Brooke's family released a statement: "It is our family's hope that by bringing this case to the forefront, our daughter will never be forgotten and justice will soon prevail for Brooke." They thanked Captain Reed and the Oconee Sheriff's Office "for keeping Brooke's case in the minds of the public." Brooke's case remains unsolved.

TIFFANY SOUERS'S MURDER

In 2006, news headlines revisited both of the unsolved Clemson coed murders. In the end, neither the deaths of Norsaadah Husain nor Brooke

Holsonback were related to what happened at the Reserve apartments, but the specter of another unsolved murder surely haunted investigators.

On the afternoon of May 26, 2006, Tiffany Marie Souers's former roommate and her roommate's boyfriend stopped by Tiffany's to return her spare key. They found the rising junior civil engineering student dead. She'd been strangled with a bikini top and left in her bedroom. The shocking discovery quickly made national headlines as Clemson students began locking their doors and keeping an eye out for strangers, while police scrambled to find whoever had disrupted the calm of a usually safe college town.

Those who knew Tiffany couldn't imagine she had any enemies. Her friends said she had an infectious laugh and was involved with her church and charitable work. The more police questioned her friends and neighbors, the clearer the picture of a kind young woman emerged. One of her roommates told Fox News that not even ex-boyfriends could be suspected; she just didn't have enemies.

Tiffany tended to be security conscious. Her ground-floor apartment was located at the rear of the complex, with a narrow, dark passageway leading to her door. At the time, the parking lot behind her apartment overlooked a neighboring construction site.

The small town and its large population of students were understandably distressed. This crime was too close to home, and as one coed said, "It could have been any one of us."

Unlike in the cases of Brooke Holsonback and Norsaadah Husain, advances in DNA technology quickly yielded matches to crimes in Florida and North Carolina and focused the investigation. Less than two weeks after the murder, on June 6, Jerry Buck Inman was arrested in Dandridge, Tennessee. Inman, a registered sex offender, traveled the Southeast working construction jobs—which is how, quite by accident, he caught sight of Tiffany Souers.

In testimony during a hearing, Inman said he'd seen Tiffany on her porch while he was working. He broke into the apartment in the early morning, when he said he didn't think anyone was home. He didn't intend to hurt anyone. But Tiffany was there alone. He got her credit cards, ATM card and her PIN number, then assaulted and strangled her, twisting a bikini top around her neck.

At the SunTrust Bank, Inman tried to use Tiffany's ATM card, but he'd forgotten her PIN number. Though he covered his face with a bandana, the camera caught the grillwork of a Chevrolet Blazer or GMC—which further linked him to the crime after he was arrested.

Highway 93 entering Clemson from Central, with a Clemson Tiger paw on the pavement pointing toward campus and downtown. *Photo by Jack Grooms.*

In 2016, the *State* newspaper named Jerry Buck Inman as one of South Carolina's seven most notorious killers, along with Susan Smith, Lee Roy Martin and Todd Kohlhepp.

Inman said he deserved to die. He pled guilty in Pickens County court in 2008, and the judge sentenced him to death. After lengthy appeals, in May 2020, a judge acting on special assignment by the South Carolina supreme court held that, even though he pled guilty, Inman's sentence should have been decided by a jury rather than by a judge. Inman sits on death row at the Broad River Correctional Institution in Columbia, awaiting a date for his resentencing hearing.

Chapter 10

THE RANDOM KILLER

When unprovoked evil intrudes into otherwise quiet, ordinary lives, the shock waves register far away from the event, alerting others to the possibility, no matter how rare, that bad things happen—bad *people* happen—to those who have done nothing to deserve it.

On June 7, 2000, when Judy Southern got home from her job as a rural mail carrier, she had no way of knowing that Jonathan Kyle Binney was waiting inside the house she shared with her husband. She didn't know Binney, didn't know he lived only about two miles from her home and certainly didn't know what he had planned for that afternoon.

Binney had recently been arrested for sexually assaulting his three-month-old baby. His lawyer had told him that, given the charges, he was looking at a minimum of ten years in prison. Binney knew an inmate guilty of violence toward a child would not fare well inside prison. Frankly, he was scared. But he'd figured out a way to solve that problem.

Binney got a friend to sell him a handgun. He took the gun with him and went to the Cherokee County home of Judy and Allen Southern. He had randomly chosen them as his target—either Judy or Allen, it didn't matter to him which one. That first evening, he watched the house, studying their routine. He then curled up in the woods and spent the night.

The next morning, he watched the couple leave for work before he entered the house. He cut the phone lines and moved the kitchen knives and any other potential weapons where the homeowners couldn't easily find them.

For six hours, he made himself at home, fixing himself something to eat, watching TV and doing what the prosecutor later called "unspeakable things…only depraved people would do." Apparently, he lost track of time and didn't hear Judy come home. He was in the bathroom when she surprised him. Startled, she ran from the house as he shot at her. He chased her, firing the gun in her direction to "keep her scared and running," he later said.

Then he jumped on his motorized bike and took an off-road route home, disposing of the gun as he went.

Judy's husband came home from work and found her lying in the yard, unresponsive. He called police. She'd been shot in the abdomen and died later at the hospital.

The investigators searched the area, found a crumpled suicide note addressed to Binney's wife and, from that, were soon knocking on the Binneys' door with an arrest warrant for assault with intent to kill. Though they didn't have a search warrant, Mrs. Binney gave them permission to search the house, where they found Mr. Binney in the basement crawlspace.

As Binney stood in the yard talking to investigators, his wife stood on the porch talking to a lawyer on the phone. She yelled at Binney: "Don't say anything!"

Binney was explaining that he had nicotine patches stuck all over his chest because he wanted to kill himself. He later claimed he went to the Southerns' house for the same reason; he'd broken in intending to kill himself there, not to burglarize their home. If he could convince the jury he wasn't a burglar, the death penalty would no longer be an option. If he could convince the jury he wanted to kill himself, he might garner some sympathy.

Neither of those arguments proved convincing.

In 2002, the jury found him guilty of first-degree murder. The killing occurred during a burglary, which is an aggravating circumstance under South Carolina law and made the case eligible for the death penalty. The judge instructed the jury they could consider the aggravating circumstance, but they could also consider mitigating circumstances that would give Binney a sentence of life without the possibility of parole. They could even reduce his punishment "for no reason at all, other than as an act of mercy."

After deliberating, the jury recommended the death penalty, and the judge pronounced the death sentence, along with a separate sentence of life without parole for the first-degree burglary.

At the time of Binney's trial, Trey Gowdy had been serving as the solicitor—called a prosecutor or district attorney in other states—for Spartanburg and Cherokee Counties since his election in 2000. Gowdy had developed a reputation for posting wins in death penalty cases. His time as Seventh Circuit solicitor came between his time as an assistant U.S. attorney and his election to Congress in 2010.

Gowdy's career on the public stage was accompanied by plenty of colorful stories and critique. A 2016 *Rolling Stone* article referred to his "frosty head of hair that changes in cut and style and inspiration seemingly by the month" and cited *GQ*'s comparisons of his hairstyles to those of Keith Urban, Emma Watson and Draco Malfoy. The *Rolling Stone* writer likened him to Atticus Finch—but in a pink seersucker suit.

The pink seersucker suit had its own story. Gowdy told *ABA Journal* writer Randy Maniloff the suit was a special gift from the Spartanburg County Sheriff's Office. Gowdy said, "Cops don't make a lot of money. So for them to go pool their money and have a suit made—not bought, but made— for a prosecutor, you're doggone right I'm gonna wear it. No matter how ridiculous I look in it."

When he was first arrested, Binney wanted to be executed. He wanted to go to prison as a killer. Much better, by his calculus, to be a killer than a sex offender. He wanted the death penalty. He wanted to die.

Later, he changed his mind. The man who said he wanted to die rather than live in prison appealed his conviction.

He claimed his constitutional right to counsel had been violated by the investigators. But the South Carolina Supreme Court held that Binney had initiated contact with law enforcement and had not invoked his right to counsel after his arrest. He had also admitted to killing Judy Southern in two formal interviews and even wrote a letter apologizing to her husband, Allen, according to court documents.

By the time Binney's death penalty appeal won him a new hearing in 2016, Binney had changed his sexual identity. Her name now was Taylor Alex Cross.

In 2018, following a hearing on whether the trial judge's instruction about a life sentence as "an act of mercy" was confusing, forty-four-year-old Cross was sentenced to life without parole and moved from death row. In exchange, Cross had to agree to file no more appeals to either the 2002 conviction or to the punishment. Reports said because Cross identified as transgender, attorneys made handwritten changes to the agreement, recognizing the legal name change to Taylor Alex Cross and marking through the pronouns in the document, changing each one from "he" to "she."

Though the death penalty still remains a legal option in South Carolina, juries rarely use it, opting instead for LWOP—life without parole, a permanent life sentence. As part of society's changing sentiments about criminal punishment, a series of U.S. Supreme Court cases have questioned the validity of using LWOP sentences for juvenile offenders, the first move pushing against the LWOP sentencing option.

In 2009, after almost ten years as a state solicitor, Trey Gowdy announced he was stepping down. Gowdy had tried seven first-degree murder cases and gotten seven death penalty verdicts. At the same time, the death penalty was receiving increasingly sharp critique and analysis from all sides. Even among prosecutors who fight to find justice for victims' families, some had come to question the trauma that prolonged appeals inflicted on those already victimized. Gowdy said that "increasingly families are saying no to a death penalty trial."

Gowdy later told journalist Maniloff, "It takes a toll on your soul. There are no trials for good, decent or kind people in the courtroom; the trials are for those who murder, rape and commit burglaries....When evil is all you see, you fall prey to believing it is all that exists." He said he never found a theologically satisfying answer for such depravity.

Chapter 11

THE SERIAL KILLERS

For such a small state, South Carolina has hosted an unusual array of serial killers. Some captured national and international headlines; all left indelible marks on the communities they haunted.

GREENVILLE'S REEDY RIVER KILLER

Sometimes a crime grips a community because it's unconceivable—no clear motive, no pattern to who is harmed or who might be next. Upstate South Carolina has witnessed more than one of those periods when a community holds its breath, waiting for what happens next, hoping the one responsible is caught quickly but not seeing how that can happen because the killer's actions are beyond their ken and hard to predict.

In 1975, Greenville played host to just such a series of crimes. Young girls were snatched up and murdered, at first without any clues.

Friday night football was a tradition for Kathy Smith and Cynthia Jones, students at Greenville High School. On an August night in 1975, they'd made their plans for one of the first games of the season. Cynthia was living with Kathy and her family on Green Street, practically next door to the high school. Sirrine Stadium, where the Red Raiders played, was a little over a mile from the school and from their house.

Kathy Smith and Cynthia Jones attended a Greenville High School football game at Sirrine Stadium before they disappeared. *Photo by Cathy Pickens.*

The sports field was built in 1934 to accommodate growing crowds of fans for Furman College (now University) football, when its main campus was downtown. Even after the campus moved to Poinsett Highway in 1961, the Paladins continued to play football in Sirrine Stadium until 1981. Sirrine remained the home stadium for Greenville High School's Red Raiders, as well as Greenville FC soccer.

After the game, Kathy and Cynthia headed to a popular juke joint called the Drive-In on Anderson Road, maybe a half mile from their house.

Later that night, Kathy's mother, Clemilee Smith, grew increasingly worried when the girls hadn't returned. At first, some believed they'd run off, but others knew better. Kathy always let her mom know where she was and when she'd be home. She was a good student and a faithful member of Tabernacle Baptist Church.

Weeks later, a fisherman found the body of a young girl in the Reedy River, on the northern edge of its winding trip through Greenville. Farther downriver, the Reedy flows within a block of the football stadium. The body was identified as that of another missing girl and buried, but that girl surprised everyone by returning home a few weeks later.

The body was exhumed and correctly identified as Rhonda Adams, another teenager who disappeared in August, about the time Kathy and Cynthia went missing. Something terrible was happening in Greenville.

Police returned to search the thick undergrowth along the riverbanks and found two more bodies. Investigators asked Clemilee Smith to come to Greenville Memorial Hospital, where she worked preparing salads for the patients. She knew the news couldn't be good when they showed her to the morgue.

The girls were her daughter, Kathy, and Kathy's friend Cynthia.

From the beginning, Dot Butler, a Greenville police detective, doubted the two were runaways. Her experience working juvenile cases gave her a sense that Kathy and Cynthia wouldn't take off on their own.

In 1975, Butler didn't have the kinds of forensic tools investigators would later rely on, and any physical evidence had been washed away by time and bad weather. Instead, Butler relied on old-fashioned shoe leather and the relationships she'd built within the community. In 2014, she told *Greenville News* reporter Lyn Riddle, "I can't imagine how many people I talked to."

The owner of the Drive-In juke joint passed along information about a man in a gray Cadillac with *Goldie* written on the side. Goldie wore a jaunty hat, and word on the street was he lured girls out of state and prostituted them.

Following information as it led from one interview to another, Butler learned Goldie was Charles Williams. In his non-gangster life, he worked at his father's mechanic shop in Spartanburg. Police found the distinctive Cadillac hidden under brush on the father's property; *Goldie* had been removed from the side. Charles's father insisted his son wasn't Goldie.

By this time, Butler had learned enough to arrest Charles Williams for transporting minors across state lines for prostitution, but she had to work quickly to build a case for murder. She could only hold him for thirty days.

Butler discovered that Williams, the obedient son who worked with his father, had also built for himself a second, more exciting life in Greenville, prowling the nightlife and patterning himself after a guidebook written by

The Reedy River has been developed as an urban park with miles of walking trails, but the riverbanks are still wild and overgrown. *Photo by Cathy Pickens.*

a former pimp. Robert Maupin, aka Robert Beck, aka Iceberg Slim, retired from the life of a Chicago pimp after his third stint in prison, moved to Los Angeles and published the first of his books, *Pimp*, in 1967, recounting his life in 1940s and 1950s Chicago.

Charles Williams kept a copy of that book in his Greenville motel room. The book, along with conversations with women in his life, helped investigators paint a picture of Williams's "night" life.

Only later were people in the neighborhood around Green Avenue, the high school and the hospital able to piece together the places where their lives intersected with Charles Williams's life. Williams's Cadillac would be parked near the Smith house. He often loitered outside the hospital. Clemilee Smith later said she thought she'd walked past him on occasion, and she suspected he must have been the man who offered Kathy a modeling contract. Smith put her foot down about that, but her vigilance didn't save her daughter or her daughter's friend, Cynthia.

One of Williams's prostitutes told police about the night she slid into the front seat of the Cadillac and saw three girls in the backseat, unconscious. "Goldie" said they were drunk. He drove to an alley near a creek, she said. She helped him get the girls out of the car, remove their pants and shave their heads. What happened after that, she didn't know. She got back in the car, and he rejoined her later, alone.

Those three girls were the same ones later found dumped near the Reedy River.

The attorney who prosecuted Charles Williams was himself a graduate of Greenville High School. Billy Wilkins, as everyone called him, was elected solicitor for Greenville and Pickens Counties in 1974. He was later appointed to a federal district judgeship and eventually became chief judge for the federal Fourth Circuit Court of Appeals. He didn't retire as a judge, even though that is a lifetime appointment. Instead, he returned to the practice of law, trying every case with his characteristic intensity.

Williams never admitted to killing the girls and didn't testify at his trial. In April 1976, he was sentenced to die for the murders. A series of cases challenging the existing death penalty laws meant Williams would later be sentenced to three life sentences.

As Lyn Riddle reported, Williams held a series of jobs in prison, ranging from brick mason to librarian to chaplain to custodian. In 2014, when he was up for parole, Kathy Smith's mother and other family members were there to fight.

The trial of the Reedy River killer took place in the Greenville County Courthouse on East North Street. *Photo by Cathy Pickens.*

At his parole hearings, he said he "didn't mean to kill the girls. He didn't know how potent the drugs were that he gave them." They met at a club and popped some pills; he didn't know how dangerous the pills were. At that point, his story diverged from that of the former prostitute who testified against him. He said he drove them to a park known as a party spot and left them, hoping they would wake up.

Williams went to prison when he was twenty-five years old, ten years older than Kathy would have been at the time. In March 2021, at age seventy-one, he was denied parole for the nineteenth time.

THE GAFFNEY KILLERS

On February 8, 1968, the phone at the *Gaffney Ledger* office rang. Managing editor Bill Gibbons later said the call really wasn't for him, but he was the one back from lunch early, so he took it.

The caller didn't identify himself. He just said, "Take out three sheets of paper. I've got three stories for you. Write down what I tell you on each sheet."

First, he told him to write *Nancy Christine, East Smith Street.* Telling Gibbons to "listen carefully," he gave directions to a lovers' lane near Chain Gang Road.

On the second sheet, Gibbons dutifully wrote *Nancy Carol Parris, Chatham Avenue.* The directions on that sheet were to the bridge on Ford Road. "Look in the water on the downhill side. You'll find her body there."

The third sheet read *March, 1967, Jerusalem Road, Union County, Annie Louise Dedmon.* Gibbons would later learn the caller didn't have the correct name.

The caller told Gibbons, "Do not go alone."

Was the caller warning Gibbons to protect himself so he wouldn't be considered a suspect, as one reporter suggested? Not a far-fetched notion, as the story got more frightening, and the rumor mill spun wilder suspicions. Or was contacting a reporter and the sheriff a sure way to attract them to the scene, to investigate and tell the story?

"Get the sheriff to go with you and you will find two bodies at the locations I have given you. This is not a crank call."

A narrow alley led about a block from the *Ledger* office to the house that served as the jail and the home of Sheriff Julian Wright and his family. Gibbons's visit interrupted lunch. The sheriff said he doubted they'd find anything, but best check it out.

Along with a deputy, they drove first to the bridge on Ford Road—easier to look over the bridge than to traipse through thick brush to find the other scenes.

Attempts to shrug it off as a prank ended the moment they saw the nude body on the bank below, her head partially in the water. When they got closer, the bruise circling her neck was hard to miss. The autopsy would confirm twenty-year-old Nancy Parris had been raped and strangled.

They summoned more deputies, and three other reporters joined them to search the lovers' lane location described on Gibbons's first sheet of paper. The group started in the clearing where cars often parked and then spread out into the dense woods. Before long, one of the searchers yelled. They found the second victim, fourteen-year-old Nancy Christine Rhinehart—Tina, her family called her. She'd been missing for a week. She, too, had been strangled and raped.

The first known victim of the Gaffney Strangler was found in the creek under the bridge on Ford Road. *Photo by Cathy Pickens.*

The caller had gotten her address wrong; her family lived on Montgomery Street. But he had everything else correct.

Finding the woman on the third sheet of paper took a little longer because the name wasn't right, because she wasn't in Cherokee County and because she'd already been found and her husband already convicted of her murder. Roger Dedmond was ten months into his eighteen-year sentence for killing Lucille Dedmond, serving his time on the Union County chain gang.

In 1968, Gaffney and Cherokee County were known for textile mills and peach orchards. Interstate 85 had opened only four years earlier, the first interstate highway in South Carolina. It's easy to forget a time when social media didn't broadcast every rumor immediately, a time when not everyone had telephones in their houses. It's also hard to remember a time before forensic science became a household term.

As this case unfolded, news reporters would be on the crime scene serving as photographers and sometimes helping carry a body out of the woods. Physical evidence didn't yield the kind of information it does today—and citizens no longer help at crime scenes.

Three reporters quickly became involved, and all three later wrote books about the experience, providing on-the-scene information and the benefit of perspective, years removed from the rapidly unfolding horror. Tommy Martin and Bill Gibbons, editors at the *Gaffney Ledger*, and Jim Holland Jr., who was in town covering another story for the *Spartanburg Herald-Journal*, worked alongside investigators from several jurisdictions as the list of victims grew and the town grew more frightened. Looking back forty years later, Martin said the three reporters "were known and trusted by law enforcement personnel and were given almost free access at that time. They assisted police with information gathering, checking out leads, and dispelling rumors." In an understatement, he added, "The situation would've been much different if it happened today."

The journalists feared for their own families as they reported how people altered their daily lives, not knowing where the killer would strike next. What would later be most frightening was that the killer wasn't unknown at all. Plenty of people knew him. They just couldn't imagine he could be the one. No one saw a clue, not even his wife.

ALMOST A YEAR BEFORE the phone call, in May 1967, Lucille Dedmond and her husband, Roger, were partying in the bars around Gaffney—and fighting about how much he'd had to drink. After much fussing, Lucille took over the driving, with Roger snoozing in the passenger seat. Roger wanted to stop at the Donut Diner near Five Points to get coffee and a sandwich. When he came out of the diner about fifteen minutes later, the car was there but no Lucille in sight.

He made a couple of stops before heading home to wait for her. She never returned.

When her body was found, naked, in a ditch in neighboring Union County, Roger was the chief suspect. He confessed, but at trial said he didn't know how Lucille died. He'd been drinking. The jury convicted him, but because the murder showed no signs of premeditation, he was sentenced to eighteen years. Roger Dedmond was serving his time, and the case became one of those domestic tragedies that fades into the background for all except those close to it—until the phone rang at the *Ledger*.

The sheriff now mobilized his small department. They learned Nancy Parris had walked her dog to the store to get change for a ten-dollar bill and make a phone call. When she and the dog didn't return home, her husband called police. During the week Tina Rhinehart disappeared, her parents called the sheriff's office every day. They were frantic because just taking off wasn't something Tina would do.

While investigators scrambled to deal with the new murders and their remote crime scenes, the caller again dialed Bill Gibbons—this time, at his home number.

The caller focused on Lucille Dedmond. "We're going to have to do something about that man down yonder serving my sentence," he said. To prove he knew what he was talking about, he described Lucille, driving a red Ford with a burned-out left taillight, passing him at high speed on Scenic Highway 11 near Linder's Vineyard. A man—her husband, he assumed—looked to be passed out in the passenger seat.

He followed her car back toward Gaffney, where she pulled into the Donut Diner. The caller didn't explain how he got her into his car. But he was very explicit about what items she carried in her handbag, including an aluminum comb and a picture of a girl sitting on the back of a white Falcon. He called back to add that she also had grocery store trading stamps with her.

He said he killed her same as he'd killed Mrs. Parris and Miss Rhinehart. "I killed them with them all begging me not to do it." He wanted to clear Dedmond, but he wasn't about to make it easy for anyone to catch him. He wouldn't tell what he'd used to kill them or exactly where it happened because he left tire tracks in the dirt there that could help identify him. He added another chilling threat: "If they don't catch me there'll be more deaths."

As news spread—which was, after all, the killer's motive in calling a journalist—life in small-town Gaffney changed. Young women and those who loved them began taking precautions. One woman carried a shotgun to walk her children to their bus stop. No one had seen anything in any of the cases. No one knew who to trust.

Years later, in a television documentary, a Black woman said she and her friends weren't too concerned. Only white girls and women had been killed—only slender, attractive brunettes.

On February 13, 1968, that sense of safety evaporated when fourteen-year-old Opal Buckson was grabbed at her bus stop and shoved into a blue sedan. The family lived in the Mount Sinai community, and Opal and her sister walked on a rural road from their house to catch the school bus. Opal was about half a football field's distance ahead of her sister Gracie, who watched helplessly as a slender, young white man with dark hair, wearing a jacket but no hat, drove off with Opal in the trunk. Now, no women or girls were safe.

With Opal's kidnapping, even more law enforcement officers arrived in town. The FBI couldn't actively operate until she'd been missing for twenty-four hours, but the agent from Spartanburg came, along with more SLED agents, state highway patrolmen and sheriffs and deputies from the neighboring counties of Spartanburg and Union in South Carolina and Cleveland and Rutherford Counties in North Carolina.

Everyone in town was on high alert, and several joined in the search. Thanks to Opal's sister, police could broadcast a description of the dark blue sedan and the slight young man with bushy hair.

Though the chances were thin, the scores of searchers on February 14 hoped they might find Opal alive. Among the volunteers, two men joined forces at a country store to scout some woods west of Gaffney. Henry

Volunteer searchers fanned out looking for kidnapped Opal Buckson, who was found off Highway 11 toward Chesnee. *Photo by Cathy Pickens.*

Transou, golf pro at the Cherokee National Golf Club, had already driven around with the store's owner, searching his land. Transou then teamed up with Lester Skinner, a former fire warden, and drove up Scenic Highway 11 toward Chesnee in the direction of the Cowpens National Battlefield. They turned onto a dirt road into the woods about seven or eight miles from Opal's bus stop.

The two were about to give up and turn back toward the main road when Skinner pointed. "Oh, Lord, there he is."

They drove past a man standing beside a black 1957 Chevrolet pulled back onto a road in the thick trees. The bushy-haired man watched them drive past. By the time they got their car turned around, the black Chevrolet was speeding away down the dirt road. The chase was on as he made turn after turn, trying to lose his pursuers.

They got close enough for Transou to scribble the license tag number on a piece of paper he found in the glove compartment. They watched him pull up to a house and talk to a man standing in the yard. At that point, they decided to drive on and call the sheriff's office.

Deputies checked out the lead and the license plate. Tracks in the dirt showed the car had driven several yards farther down the road than where he'd been seen. The woods were too thick for anyone to come here to hunt or hike.

Back at the house where Transou and Skinner gave up the chase, the owner didn't know the man who'd pulled into his yard. The man had asked if he sold beagle puppies. The homeowner didn't and didn't know anybody who did. The stop had been designed to throw off the pursuers.

Searchers amassed in the woods where the two men had spotted the car. They found Opal's body on February 16, eight days after the phone call had led to the bodies of Nancy Parris and Tina Rhinehart. Opal was tucked into a creek bank, almost impossible to find—except by one sharp-eyed searcher, who knew a dead tree limb probably hadn't fallen onto a broken limb that still had green leaves.

In addition to being strangled and raped, Opal had also been stabbed. She likely died the day she was kidnapped three days earlier.

A friend arranged for Transou to meet with SLED's Lieutenant Dick McKinnon to tell him about the guy in the woods and their car chase. They met in a room in the rear of the Shamrock Inn, where out-of-town law enforcement had set up an impromptu office. The story of the chase hadn't made its way to McKinnon, but he had information Transou and others didn't—lots of information.

Investigators met in rooms at the Shamrock Inn, since demolished for an I-85 widening project. *Image from Google Image capture: May 2019 ©2021 Google.*

The public couldn't know how rapidly investigators were pulling together their case and how tight the net was drawing around the killer.

One of McKinnon's details became public only later, in 1993: a man approached McKinnon at the courthouse and told him he'd watched as Mrs. Parris's body was thrown off the Ford Road Bridge. The married man had been parked with his also-married girlfriend near the bridge on Wednesday night. He'd seen the 1957 black Chevrolet, the white man with thick black hair who lifted something from the trunk and threw it over the bridge. At first, he thought someone was disposing of a dead dog. When he later realized what he'd witnessed, he wrestled with how to tell local police without endangering his marriage and his girlfriend's. But the stakes in the case were high. McKinnon was from Columbia, not local. The man decided to risk telling what he'd seen.

McKinnon now had the tag number and the same physical description from four witnesses—Opal's sister, Transou, Skinner and the man at the bridge.

The license plate number gave them a name: thirty-year-old Lee Roy Martin. Those who knew him couldn't see him as a killer, even though he'd served a year on the county chain gang for assault and battery with intent to kill. When he was nineteen, he'd hit a girl on the head while they were off in the woods a half mile from his mother's house.

But now, people knew him as a first-shift worker at the Musgrove textile mill. He'd once driven for Red Top Taxi. A nice guy. Married. Three small children. Lived in a small wood-frame house on Second Avenue.

Despite his generally good reputation with his neighbors and coworkers, the evidence was tying Lee Roy Martin to the murders, bit by bit.

SLED set up a command center, complete with private telephone lines, in the back room at the Colonial Restaurant on Cherokee Avenue, two blocks from Martin's house. Officers parked their cars on the opposite side of the restaurant, so they weren't easily seen from the direction of Martin's house.

From the Colonial Restaurant's rooftop, hidden behind the air-conditioning unit, they watched the house twenty-four hours a day. They watched Martin wash his car in the front yard and clean handprints from the rear window. They watched him when he stopped in the Majestic Café every morning on the way to work to read the Spartanburg newspaper before his shift started. They followed him to Musgrove Mill and waited for his shift to end.

They watched him drive to his mother-in-law's house, take off all four tires and replace them with four tires from a jacked-up junker in the backyard. He put his tires in the trunk of the old car and left them there.

Though the police carefully built their case, the public never heard most of the detail because it wasn't needed at his trials.

On February 16, as soon as word came the searchers had found Opal's body that morning, three officers went to the textile plant to arrest Lee Roy Martin. They found him outside the plant's card room, taking a noon smoke break with some coworkers. The arrest warrant charged him with Opal Buckson's murder. Officers transported him straight to Columbia, where he could be questioned and kept away from the growing anger in Cherokee County.

TWELVE DAYS LATER, ON February 28, 1968, Roger Dedmond left the county prison camp. One year to the day after his wife's body was found, two weeks after Opal Buckson's kidnapping and more than six months before Lee Roy Martin went to trial, Roger Dedmond was a free man. He'd served ten months for killing his wife. He reunited with his two-year-old son and his family, who'd stood by him through the ordeal.

Lee Roy Martin's first trial started on September 16, 1968, for the murder of Opal Buckson. Given the eyewitnesses who saw him kidnap Opal and

The murder trials of Lee Roy Martin were held at the Cherokee County Courthouse in Gaffney. *Photo by Cathy Pickens.*

saw him near the spot where her body was found, her case had more direct evidence than the others.

Before the court proceedings began that day, Bill Gibbons was allowed to talk to Lee Roy Martin at the county jail (and sheriff's house). Martin suspected they wanted Gibbons to confirm that Martin's was the voice he'd heard on the phone. But Gibbons had his own unanswered questions.

In his book, Gibbons recounted his pretrial conversation with Martin: "Well, you finally got your wish. Dedmond is free and he has his life back with his son."

"Yeah," Martin said, "but they really didn't want to admit it. I can't believe that sorry excuse for a trial. Anybody should have seen that that man was not guilty." Martin had attended the Dedmond trial, which he said changed him. He explained the trial was so upsetting it made the bad side of him push away his good side.

When Gibbons asked why he admitted he picked up Lucille Dedmond at the Donut Diner, Martin said he didn't know who might've seen him there, so he might as well admit it rather than later be caught in a lie. Throughout, he'd been careful about witnesses and tire tracks. Even while brazenly committing daytime crimes, he'd tried to cover his movements.

As cautious as he was, Martin also enjoyed the thrill. He told McKinnon that after he'd attacked Lucille Dedmond, he was almost out of gas and had to stop. He remembered thinking that "Mrs. Dedmond's head was only about two inches away" from the gas nozzle as the attendant pumped the gas.

Why would Lucille Dedmond get into a car with a strange man and leave her car and her drunk husband? Fact was, Lucille didn't get into a car—she got into a cab. At the time of her murder, Lee Roy Martin was driving a Red Top cab.

Martin's court-appointed defense attorneys, H.R. Swink and C.D. Padgett, chose to try the case without a jury in front of Judge James Morrison of Georgetown. The move surprised court-watchers and drew criticism. Many felt the community needed to hear the facts, to face the killer, to see justice served. After the trial, many also criticized the judge's decision to sentence Martin to life rather than the electric chair.

The defense attorneys went on to waive jury trials in the remaining three cases. The same evidence was succinctly presented to the judge; the verdicts were the same.

After facing such unnerving fear and losing young women in such horrifying ways, the community felt a need for vengeance that wasn't assuaged in these bench trials.

And to the surprise of some, SLED agents were among those testifying for a recommendation of mercy, to avoid the death penalty, because Martin provided evidence to prove the four cases. As soon as he was arrested, Martin was held at Central Prison in Columbia for his own protection. At trial, officers testified they'd spirited him back to Cherokee County during that time so he could show them the scattered locations where he had discarded victims' personal items.

In the one time he took the stand during his four trials and again in his one prison interview, with Jim Holland, Martin claimed he didn't know anything about those locations, that officers already had a map to the body of Nancy Parris's poodle and Tina Rhinehart's pocketbook and Opal Buckson's shoe and clothes, thrown down a well. He said he was just along for the ride and didn't know anything about those items. He complained to Holland that he hadn't trusted the officers, that he'd been too afraid to contradict anything they said. He'd been in the woods to meet a "lady friend" when Transou and Skinner saw him, and he raced off because he thought one of the men might be her husband.

He also told his mother and others that he didn't kill, that another part of him did, a part of him that took over and he couldn't "put it back."

The intense news coverage of the trial included a photograph of officers blocking Tina Rhinehart's sister from getting to Martin as he was escorted from the courtroom to the car that would take him back to Columbia. The photo captured her leaning forward, her finger pointing. Martin, wearing sunglasses, reportedly just smiled.

At the time, few knew that more than Tina's death sparked her family's anger. As Tommy Martin (no relation to Lee Roy Martin) reported, Lee Roy made a habit of paying his respects to his victims' families. He'd visited Tina's family home as she lay in her casket in the living room where friends came to visit and pay their respects.

"She sure is a pretty girl. I don't see how anybody could have done this to her," he said to the family as he stood by her body.

The family had also received strange, threatening phone calls and hang-ups before Tina was kidnapped, so the anger and grief had built over time for them.

Officer Carl Hughey, who knew Martin well, lived next door to Nancy Parris's house. Hughey saw Martin crossing the lawn to pay his respects to her family. Whether Martin attended Opal Buckson's funeral was rumored but not confirmed.

The closeness, the familiarity of the killer with Gaffney and the victims he killed remained one of the real horrors of the case. Sending Roger Dedmond to prison had been easy—he'd been drunk and couldn't deny he killed Lucille. But when the others disappeared, when their bodies were found, Gaffney citizens had to look around and wonder: Do I know the killer? In the end, plenty of them did—and never suspected him.

Even though he was no faceless stranger wandering through town, killing and moving on, Martin fit the technical definition of a serial killer: someone who has killed three or more people. But he was no stereotypical unemployed, isolated loner. He was a family man, living with his wife and three kids and working his job at a local textile mill. Most considered him a good guy. Gaffney was glad to have a face—even though it was too familiar—to put on the killer so it could move past those anxious days haunted by the Gaffney Strangler.

In state prison, Martin had difficulties with other inmates and was segregated in the Mental Ward for his safety. But when he petitioned to be allowed to exercise outside in the prison yard, he was moved back to the general population. On May 31, 1972, a fellow inmate fatally stabbed him in the chest. The inmate, Kenneth Marshall Rumsey from Pickens, was serving time for another murder and killed himself five years after he murdered the Gaffney Strangler.

A DIFFERENT MONSTER

Defying the odds for a small community, Gaffney again hosted a deadly terror. Forty years after the Strangler, a spree killer came to town.

On June 27, 2009, sixty-three-year-old Kline Cash was found dead in the living room at his peach farm of a gunshot wound.

On Wednesday, July 1, mother and daughter Hazel Linder, eighty-three, and Gina Linder Parker, fifty, were found in their house, bound and shot. On Thursday, father and daughter Stephen Tyler, forty-eight, and Abby, fifteen, were shot while closing their family furniture and appliance store near downtown Gaffney. Abby survived for two days in the hospital before she died.

The entire region was on alert. This killer had acted quickly, violently and with no clear pattern or reason. He didn't sneak into people's homes at night but acted in the open, in broad daylight. Pawnshops were almost cleared of guns. Fourth of July celebrations were canceled or curtailed. Wanted posters with a rough sketch of the suspect were plastered in store windows all over town. The series of funerals were sad tributes to five people whose family and friends loved them.

On July 6, just over the state line in Gaston County on Spencer Mountain Road near Dallas, North Carolina, a man saw a Ford Explorer parked at an abandoned house. He called police. With the recent events in Gaffney, one just couldn't be too careful.

Officers responded at two thirty in the morning and found three people at the house. As they asked questions and ran checks on the three, they realized the man who'd just provided them a false name had a twenty-five-page rap sheet. Patrick Tracy Burris, forty-one, had committed multiple crimes in five states. After his parole in April 2009, he never bothered checking in with his parole officer. He just vanished.

But now, here he was. Police didn't ask any more questions. One officer pulled a stun gun to arrest him. Burris fired first, hitting the officer in the leg. The other officers shot and killed the six-foot-seven, 280-pound felon.

Burris's gun was the one used in the Gaffney killing spree. Items belonging to the victims were in his SUV. Burris was dead, and no one could ask him to explain what had spurred him to kill five people in as many days. He'd been on a drug binge, but he stole unusual items from his victims and left behind money and valuables, leading investigators to speculate he operated more from meanness than a need for drug money.

In trying to understand what happened, why Burris chose these people and this end, the investigation provided some answers but still couldn't explain much. The night Stephen and his daughter Abby Tyler were shot in their family furniture store, Burris started partying with a couple. The couple said later he just wouldn't stop watching the national coverage of the three killings and joking about it. That made the couple uncomfortable, but still they suggested using an abandoned house that belonged to their family as a crash pad—the house across the road from the vigilant neighbor, who alerted police.

People who'd known Burris, in prison and on the outside, talked to reporters and investigators as they pieced together his lengthy record. One officer described him: "He was unpredictable. He was scary. He was weird." That was all the explanation anyone was going to get.

Everyone was looking for answers to the big question: Why the spree killing? One expert explained to a *Charlotte Observer* reporter that a spree killer—defined as one who kills at least two people at different locations without a cooling-off period—knows he's going to get caught. A spree killer like Burris doesn't want to go back to prison, so he decides to go out big. "He decides he's going to have a heyday. You can't run around in a noticeable van, with a noticeable face, and not expect people to find you."

IN AN INTERVIEW FOR *Newsweek* in 2009, after Burris's killing spree, journalist Bill Gibbons reflected on the two crimes that shocked Gaffney. The search for the killers each lasted about nine days. "But the old one seemed longer to me," Gibbons said.

Gibbons felt Martin had a split personality—which was something others mentioned in the days after his arrest, with his comments about a separate part of himself he could no longer control. He told Gibbons that "fat and ugly women, they don't need to fear me, and the men don't need to fear me either."

As for how Burris ended up in Gaffney, Gibbons said that was "pure bad luck." If Burris was coming from Gastonia, he simply pulled off the exit

The Peachoid water tower on I-85 is a Gaffney landmark. *Photo by Jp Valery on Unsplash.com.*

to Highway 11; all the murders happened on or near Highway 11. If he'd driven farther and exited the interstate "on 5, he would have gotten people in Blacksburg, or on 74, it'd have been Shelby or Kings Mountain." For Burris's victims, Gaffney was just the luck of a tragic draw.

Gaffney, current population thirteen thousand, and Cherokee County, population fifty-four thousand, are unlikely places to host two terrifying murderers. Fortunately, Gaffney is better known for its cameo appearances in *House of Cards* on Netflix and for its Peachoid, the enormous water tower designed and painted like a peach to celebrate the county's cash crop—though some think it looks like giant buttocks mooning drivers on busy Interstate 85. Still, it's a much more cheerful image of Gaffney and its small-town quirkiness than the headlines of separate nightmares, forty years apart.

TODD KOHLHEPP

In late 2016, international headlines began to spread with Woodruff and Chesnee datelines, towns little known outside of South Carolina. With the shocking revelations, a *Rolling Stone* headline asked the key question: "Who is Todd Kohlhepp, Accused South Carolina Serial Killer?"

Somehow, Todd Kohlhepp didn't quite fit the serial killer stereotype. His story garnered attention in part because his alter ego was a successful real estate entrepreneur, because his capture solved a long-unsolved quadruple murder and because his downfall came in the form of a resilient, resourceful young woman he'd chained in a shipping container for two months.

Also surprising was the information the killer and his mother provided. In a nationally broadcast interview, his mother talked about Kohlhepp's younger years. Add his voluble willingness to confess in detail about his murders, and the public learned far more about Todd Kohlhepp than it usually knows about a serial killer.

And yet questions remain.

STORIES ABOUT ANY CRIME start at different points in time: when the crime was committed, when it was discovered, when the pieces came together for investigators—and further back, deep within the criminal's or the victims' childhoods. In some cases, those points in time reveal themselves in a neat, linear fashion. In others, as with Todd Kohlhepp, the revelations took more than a decade and came with surprising switchbacks.

Kohlhepp's public story started in Arizona in 1986, when he was fifteen and arrested for kidnapping and raping a fourteen-year-old neighbor. When questioned, he admitted he'd put a gun to her head, walked her the short distance to his home and assaulted her. He was charged as an adult and served fourteen years in prison.

At the time, his mother stood by him, saying he wasn't a bad boy. Yet later, in an interview, she told about his displeasure with her when he wanted to live with his dad in Arizona. To make him feel more content, the single mom worked and saved to buy him a set of bedroom furniture, thinking the gift would appease him. He took a hammer to the furniture to let her know what he thought of that gesture. After that, he moved to Arizona.

His lawyer in the Arizona rape case later said he had concerns about Kohlhepp's "future relationships with women," that he was "screwed up." *Greenville News* reporter Tim Smith wrote that Kohlhepp's probation officer saw little remorse or empathy in him. His juvenile record said: "Behaviorally, he is demanding, self-centered and likely attempts to force others to do what he wants in order to meet his own needs."

Decades later, former FBI profiler John Douglas said teenaged Kohlhepp's first arrest came at a time when proper intervention might have altered his path. His victims would later understand too well the implications of his lack of empathy. Still, nothing suggested he would turn into a sadistic serial killer.

In the 2000s, no one who worked with Todd at his Spartanburg County TKA Real Estate company knew much about that earlier part of his life, though he did bring up his history as a sex offender. To obtain his real estate license, he'd lied about his conviction, and by the time background checks were required, his license was grandfathered. He later said one competitor did mail letters to potential clients to alert them, to harm his business.

Other behavior hinted at reasons for concern. Kohlhepp frequented the Waffle House in Roebuck, not far from his house, where the female waitstaff felt so uncomfortable with his large tips and his attempts to get them to come to his house that a man was assigned as his regular server.

For victims, their stories started with innocent encounters, such as those at the Waffle House or when Kohlhepp hired someone to clean his real estate properties—ordinary business engagements, or so they seemed.

Authorities joined the story at different points, first investigating the unsolved murder of four people in a motorcycle shop in Chesnee, later looking for two sets of missing couples. Connections weren't initially clear. After all, the killings were thirteen years apart.

In August 2016, Kala Brown, who'd known Kohlhepp for a few years through a mutual friend, took a job cleaning houses for his company. On August 31, she invited her boyfriend, Charles David Carver, to help her with a job on Kohlhepp's ninety-five-acre property near Woodruff. Kohlhepp greeted them with two guns, firing three shots into Carver's chest.

He later told Kala the best way to control a person was to take away someone they loved.

Kohlhepp immediately shackled Kala in a metal shipping container and held her prisoner.

As days and weeks passed, Kala's and Charlie's family and friends were frantically trying to get in touch with them. When they found Kala's dog without food or water in the Anderson County apartment the couple shared, they knew something was wrong. Kala treasured her dog. The family reported her missing on September 5, Labor Day.

Though their families couldn't find them, Charlie's Facebook posts began announcing the two had married, bought a house, were expecting a child. Messages asked a friend of Charlie's for money for drugs, even though he wasn't known to use. Suspecting a hack, police sought warrants for the missing couples' Facebook accounts, but the warrants weren't authorized until mid-October.

On October 18, two detectives from Anderson County brought a lead to the Spartanburg Sheriff's Office from those warrants. They had a tip about Kala Brown and a cell phone ping near one hundred wooded acres in Woodruff, a small town near Spartanburg. The only property of that description belonged to a businessman who drove a BMW sports car: Todd Kohlhepp. His phone records showed he and Kala had been in contact when she vanished. That provided enough probable cause for a search warrant for his house in Moore and his Woodruff property. Sheriff's deputies hit both on the same day.

On November 3, investigators roaming around Kohlhepp's secluded property found a large shipping container, the kind hauled on tractor-trailers and loaded onto cargo ships. As they worked to remove the five locks, one searcher called for silence. They heard someone inside calling for help.

A police body camera recorded her rescue. Kala was chained in the rear of the hot, airless metal container, inside what looked like a shark cage. She immediately began telling her rescuers about Kohlhepp, about watching him shoot Charlie, about her two months in captivity.

The investigators were as relieved as Kala's family and friends—and as surprised as the rest of the world that they'd found her alive. Spartanburg County heriff Chuck Wright later told *48 Hours* he asked Kala if he could pray with her before she got in the ambulance—a prayer of thanksgiving.

On the property, officers found Charlie's car hidden under brush and the graves of three people.

Kala provided investigators a detailed account of her time with Kohlhepp: what he told her about his other victims and his intentions for their future together in the house he would build for her, where she would continue to be his prisoner. Kala managed to earn his trust, though she didn't know until later he had already dug another grave next to Charlie's.

As they rescued Kala from her prison, other investigators were knocking at Kohlhepp's two-story home in the Moore community in Spartanburg County, a quiet neighborhood of $200,000 homes. He'd lived and worked out of his house there for about ten years. Body camera footage recorded their encounter, giving the public its first glimpse of the three-hundred-pound, soft-bellied forty-five-year-old suspect and his calm, matter-of-fact reaction to his arrest in the front hallway of his home.

After his arrest, Kohlhepp told Sheriff Wright he was willing to talk, but he asked for three favors. He wanted to talk to his mother, so she wouldn't have to hear it on the news first. He also wanted to give her a photograph and transfer money into a college fund for a friend's child.

Kohlhepp ran his real estate office from his house on Windsong Way in Moore, South Carolina. *Photo by Cathy Pickens.*

He then proceeded to give investigators a chilling, hours-long interview. He confirmed Kala Brown's story about Charlie Carver's murder. He confessed to killing another missing couple, Johnny and Meagan Coxie, who had disappeared in December 2015. The three were buried in the graves on his property.

Kohlhepp met Meagan when she was working at the nearby Waffle House and offered her work cleaning his houses, mirroring his interaction with Kala and Charlie. He killed Johnny and held Meagan prisoner for about a week before he killed her around Christmas Day in 2015. He buried her beside Johnny.

Kohlhepp's mother, Regina Tague, talked openly to the press and did what any mother would do: she defended her son. She acknowledged he'd admitted killing Charlie, "because [Charlie] got nasty, smart-mouthed." But he told her he'd taken care of Kala, holding her hostage because he didn't know what else to do: she'd seen him shoot her boyfriend.

Even as she tried to explain the inexplicable, Tague shed tears for the victims. To CBS's David Begnaud, she said, "I know how bad they've hurt all this time. And they've all lost someone they love so dearly. And I am so sorry that it was my son that hurt them."

As his accounts of his crimes unfolded and as others who knew him spoke, one telling element emerged: Kohlhepp couldn't stand to feel put down or insulted—a hallmark of his personality.

Drawing conclusions about the "usual" serial killer is like describing the "usual" schoolteacher or "usual" short-order cook. Some serial killers never speak about their crimes, keeping the details locked inside for their own purposes. Others talk only with conditions or to win a concession. Some, with only the slightest provocation, talk and talk and talk, recounting every element of their crimes in well-remembered detail.

Todd Kohlhepp was a talker. In hours of taped interviews with Spartanburg sheriff's investigators, with his hulking shape in jail garb hunched over the interrogation room table, he seemed to enjoy having an audience. After sharing encyclopedic details about each of his crimes, he delivered a shock to Sheriff Wright. He admitted to four additional murders, reaching back to 2003—a case involving a shooting at a Chesnee motorcycle shop, killings Wright had tried to solve for thirteen years.

ON NOVEMBER 6, 2003, Scott Ponder, the thirty-year-old owner of Superbike Motorsports; his mother and part-time bookkeeper, Beverly Guy; mechanic Chris Sherbert and service manager Brian Lucas were found shot to death in the Chesnee shop. The case had been featured on *Unsolved Mysteries* and *America's Most Wanted*, one of the most high-profile unsolved cases in the Upstate.

The case was so dissimilar to what happened with the victims in the woods that the sheriff was left to wonder if Kohlhepp really committed the Superbike murders—or was he just building himself up, enjoying regaling investigators with his tales?

Kala said he bragged to her about Superbike, too—how he'd "cleared that building in under thirty seconds," how he wasn't just a serial killer but a mass murderer, too.

Kohlhepp repeated his boast in his interview with Spartanburg investigator Tom Clark, about how quickly he'd moved from the back of the shop to the front door. He told him the makes of the two handguns he carried, the ammunition loaded in each and in what order he killed the people in the shop that day, pleased with his plan of attack and his "tactical reload" skill. He also described where the shots hit each victim, the kind of detail investigators often hold close and away from the media as a way to test those who want to make false confessions.

Before Kohlhepp's confession, investigators had no active leads. They had no robbery. No clear motive. They had already looked into any possible motive against everyone in the shop. They investigated the shop owner's friend Noel Lee, who found the bodies and called 911 when he stopped by the store that afternoon. Sometimes the 911 caller is involved, so investigators didn't ignore that possibility.

Based on an anonymous tip, they also investigated the rumor that Scott's wife, Melissa, had been unfaithful. Seven months after Scott's death, Melissa had a son. Investigators surreptitiously got the baby's DNA from a discarded diaper. A lab test showed her newborn was not Scott's. When Melissa insisted they'd made a mistake, they ran another test with another exemplar from the baby. The results were the same.

Melissa Ponder told *48 Hours* that she and Scott had been thrilled about the pregnancy, and Scott had gone with her for the first ultrasound—just two days before his murder. For the grief-stricken mom to now be forced to defend herself against charges of infidelity and suspicion of murder only compounded her tragedy—until the lab discovered it had mixed up the exemplar of Scott's DNA with one of his employees' samples.

At least now Melissa knew she was no longer a suspect. Still, the Ponder family had lost a mother and son. The families of Brian Lucas and Chris Sherbert also lived with the grief and unanswered questions.

With the investigation stalled, Detective Sergeant Allen Wood approached former FBI profiler John Douglas after a university lecture in Upstate South Carolina. Could he provide insights into the kind of person they should be looking for? Reviewing the file, Douglas said the attack was a mission against the shop, not against a particular individual. Even though they found two different shell casings in the shop, one person—likely an unhappy customer or employee—was angry with the shop itself, and this was revenge, righting some wrong.

The investigators had considered it could've been a disgruntled customer, but they didn't contact former customers until the tenth anniversary of the massacre. When Kohlhepp got his letter asking about his transaction with Superbike, he simply didn't respond.

When he told his mother he'd committed those murders, the theme was similar to his other crimes: he was angry because he felt ridiculed. He'd

Superbike Motorsports closed after the murders. *Photo by Cathy Pickens.*

bought a motorcycle from the shop but didn't know how to ride it. He said they'd laughed and "made jokes at him," his mother said. He waited, went back later and took his revenge.

IN 2017, A YEAR after Kala's ordeal, Kohlhepp pleaded guilty and was sentenced to seven consecutive life sentences without the possibility of parole. As part of his sentencing, he told the court he'd killed no other victims. He told his mother the same thing.

In a sale of his assets to benefit his victims, Kohlhepp's house went on the market in 2019, priced at $150,000, below the market in that neighborhood.

Sitting empty takes its toll on a house. The carpet had been torn out because of the dirt and dog hair; a neighbor had been cutting the grass in the front just to keep it from being an eyesore, but the backyard was overgrown. Kohlhepp's property in Woodruff reportedly sold for $500,000. In 2018, over five hundred items from his house and property sold quickly in an online auction; signs advertising his real estate company sold for over one hundred dollars each.

From prison, Kohlhepp named former real estate office employee Gary Garrett as his biographer, but no book has yet been published. In the years before his arrest, Kohlhepp published several product reviews on Amazon that drew reporters' attention: for a padlock ("have 5 on a shipping container …won't stop them… but sure will slow them down til they are too old to care"), a knife ("havnet stabbed anyone yet…yet") and a folding shovel ("keep in car for when you have to hide the bodies and you left the full size shovel at home").

While in prison, Kohlhepp provided a handwritten foreword for an e-book written by another inmate on how to "pen pal a serial killer." His foreword said the prison mail room was flooded with correspondence for him, much of which he didn't receive because writers didn't know the rules, and he recommended the e-guide for "anyone interested in hearing the stories of serial killers from the very people who caused them."

While in prison, Kohlhepp communicated with Maria Awes, the investigative journalist and host of the 2019 Investigation Discovery series about him, *Serial Killer: Devil Unchained*. He told her he'd been involved in other killings, including two men in a Spartanburg apartment complex parking lot who attacked him one night; he dumped their bodies somewhere along Interstate 26 toward Columbia. He also participated, he said, in a "hunt club" in Mexico, killing drug dealers and bad guys. He had a pilot's license, so maybe he made those trips. Some of what he said about those cases could be feasible, but no one was reported missing in Spartanburg and nothing could be corroborated.

Kohlhepp was ready to claim other victims, and profiler John Douglas doesn't find it far-fetched that Kohlhepp killed others. But so far, no evidence has surfaced. In addition to his public claims, police investigated him for the November 2016 bank robbery and murders of a teller and two customers at the Blue Ridge Savings Bank in Greer but found no evidence to support a charge.

Kohlhepp likely wouldn't be linked to the four Superbike victims unless he'd admitted it—first to Kala Brown, a victim he planned to kill, and then

Blue Ridge Savings Bank off I-85 near Greer was the scene of a deadly robbery in 2016. *Photo by Cathy Pickens.*

to the officer recording his confession. The secret serial killer had three additional bodies and a kidnapping victim alive to tell her tale, all while operating a successful real estate business and living in a nice house in a quiet neighborhood.

Chapter 12

HOMETOWN CRIMES

C ivic boosters have longed billed Oconee County as South Carolina's Golden Corner. It is, in fact, a corner—the upper westernmost corner of the piece-of-pie-shaped state, wedged against the borders of North Carolina and Georgia. Those familiar with the area may wonder why it's not part of western North Carolina or maybe northeast Georgia, a conversation (or tussle) that started as early as 1787.

Northern Spartanburg, Greenville, Pickens and Oconee Counties lie in the foothills of the Blue Ridge Mountains, a section of the Appalachian chain. The hilly country offers scenic vistas, waterfalls, land difficult to farm, deep forests and a history of moonshiners and staunch individualists. Walhalla, Oconee's county seat, is my hometown.

The Revenuers

What comes as no surprise to longtime residents is that the Golden Corner's civic boosterism was an attempt to distinguish it from the Dark Corner, a historic bootlegging haven. Cherokee Foothills Scenic Highway 11 now cuts through what was once the hidden heart of the Dark Corner.

The boundaries of the Dark Corner vary according to who is describing it. For some, it is upper Greenville County, bordered by the Old Tugaloo Road and the Middle Tyger River. Others consider it a much broader area,

As this 1909 *Puck* illustration showed, the battle between moonshiners and tax-collecting revenue agents was both fun and deadly serious. *Courtesy of Library of Congress.*

incorporating the Blue Ridge in South Carolina and parts of North Carolina and Georgia. Bootleggers likely weren't concerned with map locations as much as they were with good water sources, passable roads and secluded spots in the woods.

Forested mountains provided plenty of cover f illicit stills, and land ill-suited to large-scale farming operations provided ample opportunity for turning corn into liquor, an easily transported cash crop.

In South Carolina, moonshining wasn't limited to the mountains. The swamps near Charleston also provided good places to hide a still. Charleston was a thirsty market, and the Charleston *News & Courier* became an advocate for the state's moonshiners in the late 1800s.

Mountain moonshiners also found ready markets, especially in Greenville and other Upstate cities, but in the decades after the Civil War, along came the revenuers. The alcohol tax contributed a healthy chunk of the postwar federal budget.

Deputy U.S. Marshal W.B.F. Corbin was a relentless seeker and destroyer of illicit stills in Oconee County. As early as 1899, local correspondents for the *Keowee Courier* reported his activities: "Look out moonshiners! Corbin will get you sure!" the newspaper columnist from the Little River community warned in February 1909.

A month later, Corbin deputized his half brother Chris D. Corbin to help him make an arrest. A man had vandalized a mailbox, and they went to his house off the Westminster Highway to arrest him.

The prime witness to the subsequent melee was twelve-year-old Jesse Gibson, who lived on the other side of Westminster. He and his brother were visiting at Bale Palmer's house when the lawmen arrived at the door after sundown. When the knock came, the family was gathered in the front room around the woodstove, Jesse said: the family patriarch, Baylus "Bale" Palmer; his son, Charlie Palmer, and daughter, Lou Belcher; and Bob Belcher, Lou's son and Bale's grandson.

Before "old man" Bale Palmer opened the door, the others urged Bob to climb into the loft. Lou kept at her work piecing a quilt to keep things looking homey.

The two officers shone a lantern around the room and saw Bob's foot hanging down. One witness said Corbin stood on the woodstove to pull Bob out of the loft. Lou and her brother, Charlie, joined their dad in trying to free Bob from the officers.

The Corbins carried only pistols, young Jesse said, but he had seen four other guns inside the house.

A shot was fired, and Jesse and his brother took off running up the hill behind the house. They could see and hear part of the fight that spilled out onto the front porch and into the yard—including at least four more gunshots.

Jesse later told the coroner's jury that, at the end of it, he returned to the house. He didn't know if the officers were dead; he just knew they were lying quietly under an apple tree and that no one approached them.

Jesse testified that Lou, the quilter, was shot in the hip. Bale was shot in the hand. He said Lou told him to go to town with Bale to get the doctor and the sheriff, that "them devils was laying out there like they was dead, but they was not."

The newspaper later reported both Corbin brothers had gaping wounds to their chests from shotgun blasts.

The family claimed one of the Corbins fired first and set the bed on fire, even though the bedding showed no sign of burning. The sheriff found no wound where Bob said he'd been shot in the hand and couldn't see where Charlie claimed one of the Corbins hit him in the head with a stick of firewood.

In Deputy U.S. Marshal Corbin's pocket were two papers: a warrant, sworn out by the rural mail carrier J.C. Garrison for the arrest of Bob Belcher for mutilating a mailbox, and the commission for his half brother as a deputy marshal.

Lou and one of the men told the sheriff the Corbins showed up and "got to cussing and rearing around and killed themselves." No one in the house saw who killed the Corbins—but if someone had, they said, it was in self-defense.

The Palmers and Belchers were all charged with murder.

Four months later, on Monday, July 5, crowds filled the courthouse grounds trying to get seats when the trial started. On the first day, the jury heard from more than a dozen witnesses. The next day, Bob Belcher took the stand and made headlines around the state with a simple sentence: "Yes, I killed the Corbins." He shot both at close range, killing them instantly, to protect his mother, Lou.

Bob's story didn't quite match the testimony of other witnesses. He said he didn't know why the Corbins were there, only that when his grandfather "unbuttoned" the door, "the old one" (Marshal Corbin) came in with his pistol cocked and started looking through all the rooms. Belcher said he could've leapt out of the window, but he just "backed into a room on the left."

Lou, according to Bob, took on Marshal Corbin, telling him to get off the stove and quit looking in the loft, "as we had stolen nothing." She told him he couldn't walk around their house with his pistol cocked. Corbin just kept answering, "That's all right." Then Corbin confronted Bob Belcher with the pistol to his chest. It fired when Uncle Charlie pushed it away. Bob said, "He wanted to kill me, but did not have time to fire."

At that point, Belcher's testimony got crazy, with the Corbins shooting and striking out with firewood and an axe and those in the house trying to defend themselves. Belcher's story of self-defense in the face of "illegal invasion of a man's house and firing to kill all the defendants" didn't hold up well under a "truly" grueling cross-examination, which "badly shattered" his testimony.

Although Bob told the jury he had no idea why Corbin was at the house, Bob would've expected a warrant against him for firing a weapon into a mailbox. Though a mailbox was federal property, sending a federal officer and a deputized backup to arrest a mailbox vandal might seem extreme.

Left: Marshal W.B.F. Corbin and his half brother Chris D. Corbin were buried in Westview Cemetery behind St. John's Lutheran Church. *Photo by Cathy Pickens.*

Below: The graves in Westview Cemetery now sit in view of the new Oconee Law Enforcement Center. *Photo by Cathy Pickens.*

However, a hint at the real motive came in Bale Palmer's reply to Corbin's knock on his door that evening. Young Jesse testified that Bale told Corbin to "get away from there right now; there were no still about there."

Marshal W.B.F. Corbin was, after all, a revenuer, and still-busting had a long and danger-fraught history. According to the Charleston *Post and Courier*, "Moonshiners vigorously defended their territory, both against government agents—called 'revenuers'—and their rivals. Shootouts occurred often."

The Palmers, apparently, were moonshiners, and each side understood the role the other played. Vandalizing the mailbox was perhaps the Palmer/Belcher clan's way of retaliating against the government for the destruction of a still.

The jury got the case late in the afternoon. Speculation among the court-watchers as to the possible verdict ranged from all guilty to some guilty to all set free. The verdict came before noon the next day, and it fell somewhere in the middle of the range of predictions: Bob Belcher was guilty of murder with a recommendation of mercy, with manslaughter verdicts for his three family members.

The Corbin brothers were buried at Westview Cemetery behind the Lutheran cemetery in Walhalla. Both left wives and children and a large extended family.

History depends on the reporter. According to my granny, the Corbin brothers' niece, her uncles were "shot off their horses and left laying in the front yard." The descendants of the Palmers and Belchers undoubtedly have their own passed-along version.

Moonshine Robin Hood

As with other lawbreakers, a cult of admiration can grow up around moonshiners. For Upstate South Carolina in the late 1800s, the nationally known renegade hero was Lewis Redmond.

In the Carolinas, moonshining was more family business than colorful Chicago-style underworld gangster activity. Years before Prohibition, the 1909 *Keowee Courier* ran a small piece about child moonshiners imitating their elders. The reporter said two boys and a girl, ages five to ten, were making brandy with a "wooden bucket, a paint can, and a poplar limb bored out and shaped like a 'worm.'" (A "worm" is typically a coiled metal pipe submerged in a box of cold water to condense the hot alcohol vapor into liquid.) The children also knew enough to take off into the woods as soon as the revenuers appeared.

Near the end of the nineteenth century, Lewis Redmond cut a wide swath through Pickens and Oconee Counties in South Carolina, as well as western North Carolina and northeast Georgia. Separating the facts of Redmond's life from the fiction written about him by enterprising dime novelist Edward B. Crittenden was difficult. In several books, Crittenden made Redmond into a classic American frontier good guy who found himself righteously on the wrong side of unjust laws and the federal tax agents. For readers, the myth-sized heroics and flamboyant escapades became the real Redmond.

From what's known about him, Redmond was born in Swain County, North Carolina, and learned the moonshine trade from some of the best in the business. Selling 'shine was an accepted supplement to many a mountain farmer's livelihood, but after the Civil War, the federal alcohol tax was as high as two dollars per gallon, and federal tax agents—the revenuers—moved into the moonshine-rich "hollers" with a vengeance. Redmond enlarged his own myth by crusading against the injustice of taxing poor Southern mountain folk more than they could rightly pay, just because they were trying to feed their families. The twenty-one-year-old—tall, handsome and fearless—easily fit the role of Victorian bad-boy antihero.

On March 1, 1876, as Redmond was driving a wagon to make deliveries to customers in the North Carolina mountains, Deputy U.S. Marshal Alfred Duckworth stopped him at gunpoint and put him under arrest. As the story goes, Redmond told him he'd come peacefully, but when Duckworth lowered his gun, Redmond pulled a small derringer and fired, hitting Duckworth in the throat and killing him.

From there, Redmond's myth grew with tales of how he eluded capture against all odds and how he helped a woman in distress, whom he later married. Some of that was the invention of his putative biographer, Crittenden. But much of it was true. He did raid the homes of agents who tried to capture him—a shocking and effective deterrent to obsessive law enforcers. Redmond kept on the move with a gang of like-minded bootleggers (though not as large a gang as the myth maintained) and with the help of others who believed as he did in the unjustness of the tax laws.

In 1877, in Liberty, South Carolina, he made a daring escape from one arrest attempt. In 1879, he escaped minutes before a raid on his operation in Swain County. He was finally captured in a third raid that year, in a gun battle where he was shot thirteen times. His legend only grew when

Lewis Redmond, "king of the moonshiners," lived a quiet family life and was laid to rest in the Return Baptist Church cemetery. *Photo by Cathy Pickens.*

he survived what would have killed lesser men, but the wounds affected him for the rest of his life.

Authorities took him to Bryson City, then to Asheville to patch him up and eventually to trial in 1881 in Greenville, South Carolina, keeping him on the move to avoid a rumored rescue attempt.

Redmond served a portion of his ten-year federal sentence before President Chester A. Arthur pardoned him in 1884. He was "wheezing from a shot in his windpipe" and needed crutches from his final gun battle, but one of the women who'd advocated for his release still found him "handsome and pleasant looking, with a grave and settled expression in deep blue eyes." When she and other women met him after his transfer to the Columbia jail, they brought him clothes, toys for his children, fifty-five dollars in cash—and his unexpected pardon from the president.

Redmond returned to his family in Oconee County, where he made good use of his liquor-making reputation by running the government distillery in Walhalla. Even one of his nemeses admitted he made good liquor. He had nine children, mostly daughters, and led a quiet life until he died in 1906. His final years in Oconee County would have overlapped Marshal W.B.F. Corbin's still-busting heyday, though the two never had an "official" meeting.

A PERILOUS CAR CHASE

In 1920, the winding road between Walhalla and Stumphouse Tunnel was the scene of a car chase straight out of a Buster Keaton film. Rural county police officer J.G. Mitchell got a tip that B.O. Elrod—who happened to be a county constable—was involved in hauling illegal whisky. On May 18, 1920, Mitchell swore out a warrant for Constable Elrod and illicit activity involving his Ford roadster. The magistrate's warrant gave any officers authority to search Elrod's roadster.

The day they got the warrant, Mitchell and a state constable named Moss waited for Elrod along the road from Stumphouse Tunnel but never saw him.

Stumphouse Tunnel was intended to link the railroad from Charleston to Knoxville and points west, but the Civil War interrupted construction. In 1940, Clemson College found the humidity and temperature in the tunnel were ideal and started making its famous Clemson blue cheese. Before that, moonshiners apparently found conditions in the surrounding area ideal, too.

A week later, on June 25, Moss got word Elrod had headed up the mountain, so he and Mr. Gosnell, a federal Prohibition agent, waited on the road for Elrod to come back down.

Moss stood on the roadside, ready. When Elrod drove by, headed toward Walhalla, Moss waylaid him, yelling he had a warrant to search his car.

When Elrod didn't stop, Moss jumped on the running board of the roadster, which was moving about seven or eight miles an hour. Meanwhile, Agent Gosnell, parked up the road, saw Moss reach in the window as if to turn off the ignition, while Elrod sped up to fifteen miles an hour. Elrod managed to knock Moss off the roadster's running board.

Moss later testified he "struck me right here in the stomach like and... pretty nearly knocked the life out of me." Lying on the side of the road, Moss hollered that Elrod was carrying liquor and for Gosnell to give chase.

Gosnell pursued the car around the curves down the last steep part of the mountain into Walhalla. Elrod saw Gosnell was gaining on him and threw a package out the window. Gosnell had his gun out. Elrod finally pulled over but refused to let the officer search his car. Gosnell grabbed Elrod's arm and told him to wait until Moss arrived.

Meanwhile, Moss sat on the side of the road for ten or fifteen minutes, feeling sicker and sicker, before he vomited and lay down for a while. He flagged over a young couple for a ride into town to the doctor, leaving behind his car and his coat, with the search warrant in the pocket.

The doctor fixed up Moss, who then proceeded to where Gosnell held Elrod and his roadster. They searched the car and found no whiskey.

The alleged whiskey runner/constable sued the lawmen, claiming they had no right to arrest him or search his property because Moss didn't have the warrant on his person. He'd left it in his coat pocket in his car. Nevertheless, the court held the warrant was valid.

The confrontation on the mountain road moved to federal court in Greenville County, where Elrod sued in a civil case for false arrest and illegal search, seeking punitive damages. Elrod lost and appealed. Appellate courts, then and now, don't agree to hear every case, but Prohibition was new, and this raised questions about search and arrest that were important beyond South Carolina.

A few months later, three judges on the federal Fourth Circuit Court of Appeals in Richmond, Virginia, heard the lawyers' arguments. Elrod lost again. Even without a warrant in hand, the lawmen's actions were reasonable, given that Elrod pushed Moss off his car and threw a package from the window as he fled at ten or fifteen miles an hour down the mountain.

The Man at the Post Office

On September 4, 1968, folks around Walhalla were talking—maybe whispering, certainly shaking their heads—over the news a man had confessed to a fatal stabbing.

James "Griff" Cheek rented a little clapboard house on South Broad Street, just off Main Street and not far from the cotton warehouse for Chicopee Mill. He was known to be mean when drunk, ill-disposed to dogs trespassing on his property and a deadly good shot when the neighbor lady's chickens got into his garden. He was paying rent, he said, so it was his property, and he'd protect his vegetables.

Despite his cantankerousness, Griff had folks who looked out for him. Around 1960, he often stopped to speak to a little girl waiting in her mother's car at the post office, when their morning visits coincided. I was that little girl.

Years later, midafternoon on September 4, 1968, Mrs. Inez Smith called the police station and arranged to meet police chief Buck Crenshaw at Hardin's service station, a block from her home. She'd found a body in her neighbor's house.

When Mrs. Smith and the chief pulled into the driveway on South John Street, Griff was sitting on his front porch. "Chief," he said, "come in here and see what I found, somebody's killed Poor Ole Willie."

Willie Underwood, thirty-seven, had been disabled in a railroad accident a few years before and walked with two canes. Now, Crenshaw found him lying on the floor between the coal heater and the little cot bed. As soon as he saw the extent of Underwood's injuries, he called the Oconee County sheriff, the coroner and Dr. Julius Earle, a family doctor, who examined the body and called the hospital to send an ambulance.

Above: Post office in Walhalla where Griff Cheek made occasional morning visits. *Photo by Cathy Pickens.*

Left: This photo of the scene of the deadly stabbing appeared on the front page of the *Keowee Courier*. *Courtesy of the* Keowee Courier.

The crime scene that midafternoon was horrific, especially for Walhalla. Underwood's body, clothed in nothing but a shirt, lay in the small, litter-strewn room. Officers couldn't tell how the victim died because "hardly a place on the victim's body had not been slashed." The autopsy revealed at least three hundred stabs or cuts.

Authorities found a .32-caliber handgun in the house but no gunshot wounds, though neighbors reported hearing a couple of shots fired the night before. A large pocketknife appeared to be the weapon.

A chief deputy sheriff and a police officer drove Griff Cheek to Columbia that night to meet with a SLED agent. Cheek at first said he went that day to Seneca, a larger town about nine miles southeast of Walhalla, and discovered the body when he got home. He refused to take a polygraph test; he had a bad heart and was taking medication, which could affect the results. A couple of hours later, though, sometime after two o'clock in the morning, he said to the agent, "I want you to get a pencil and paper and take this down cause I want this to be in court just as I am fixing to tell you."

Cheek said he'd taken out his teeth and put them in salt water and lay down in the bed, with his back to Underwood. He awoke to a big light in his face and Underwood pointing a gun at him. He hit Underwood hard in the face and grabbed his knife from the table beside the bed and defended himself.

Police found that two cartridges had been fired from the pistol.

Cheek told the truth about the trip to Seneca that day. A driver for the Walhalla Taxi Service said Cheek walked up the railroad track from his house to the taxi stand and got a ride to Seneca's Gallant-Belk store. The driver said he didn't notice anything odd, just that Cheek appeared "nervous and upset."

At Gallant-Belk, Cheek said, he bought some new overalls. At the Dollar Store, he bought a shirt. Another cabdriver picked him up for his return trip to Walhalla and dropped him at the Tie Yard in West Union. He said Cheek was carrying a new Belk's bag under his arm, and the old overalls he was wearing looked like they had tar or something on them. Cheek got out of the cab and went through the trees to the railroad tracks.

Cheek's accounts of what happened to his bloody clothes weren't clear. He said he changed into his new shirt and overalls in the woods and stuffed his old clothes in the striped Belk's bag and threw them in the garbage. Then he said he changed clothes in "some honey suckles," though the honeysuckle vines weren't trampled. Then he said he dumped the clothes near the railroad track in West Union, somewhere between the Tie Yard and Reid's

Griff Cheek was buried in the cemetery at rural Wolf Stake Baptist Church. *Photo by Cathy Pickens.*

Saw Mill. The clothes were never found. In the official record, no one ever commented on what the local taxi drivers saw on a daily basis that would make a passenger in blood-covered overalls not particularly noteworthy.

Even though Cheek had changed clothes, authorities found blood on his hat, shoes and wristwatch. On his trip to Seneca, he had the cracked crystal in his watch replaced, but police found blood under the watch crystal, on the winding stem and on the back of the band.

A member of the coroner's jury asked if police had matched the blood on Cheek to Underwood's blood, but the officer said that hadn't been necessary since Cheek had confessed.

After hearing the testimony, the coroner's jury found Willie Underwood "came to his death at the hands of James E. (Griff) Cheek," and Cheek, who had served in World War II, was imprisoned for the death. He died in 1973 at age sixty-eight.

Was it a night of drinking gone wrong? Given the three hundred wounds, was it something more personal? Griff Cheek once greeted a little girl on his morning visits to the post office. Eight years later, when her dad brought home news of the stabbing—and for the decades afterward—she simply remembered him as a kind, friendly man.

THE AXE MURDER

On Wednesday, February 13, 1957, the headline on the front page of the *Keowee Courier* said, in rather small type, "Trunk Yields Body of Axe-Slain Man." Despite the small headline, the writer christened it "one of the most hair-raising horror stories to come out of Oconee County in many years." This was certainly not the daily news expected in Walhalla, no more than in any small town.

The story—and the body—didn't become public for several days. Accounts of the events were confusing. The murder happened back on February 7, in an isolated hilltop farmhouse about four miles outside Walhalla toward the Oconee Station area, near a late-1700s trading post.

Living in the small house were fifty-five-year-old Ethel Vaughn, her seventeen-year-old granddaughter Lillian Thrasher and fifty-eight-year-old Oscar Dover, who became the unfortunate resident of the "scarred old trunk."

The long-vanished farmhouse, scene of a gruesome axe murder, stood on White Cut Road outside Walhalla. *Photo by Cathy Pickens.*

Late on Monday, days after the death, Lillian caught a cab to Seneca and, asking around for a minister, found the Reverend Francis Whitmire of Corinth Baptist Church. She told him she'd thrown an axe at Dover and hit him in the head as he was turning away. She didn't mean to kill him, she said. She tried to get him to drink some water, and she bundled up her sweater and put it under his head, but he didn't move again after he fell.

At the coroner's inquest, Dover was described as being small in stature, weighing less than 140 pounds. Lillian somehow tumbled him into a trunk—though later, under questioning, she couldn't convincingly describe how a slender, 115-pound girl who'd "been crippled in one foot since birth" managed that. She left the lid open, thinking he would come to. When he didn't, she forced the lid closed and dragged the trunk into a closet in the four-room farmhouse.

Lillian then reported Dover missing to police, saying he "had left home Thursday and simply had not returned." Officers searched the area but found no sign of Dover.

When she later confessed to Reverend Whitmire, he took her to Sheriff L.T. McLane. Two deputies were dispatched to the farm. They had to move a dresser from in front of the closet door, where they found the scene just as Lillian had described, with the added horror that the smell of decomposition filled the house and was "simply enough to stifle a man" inside the closet. Opening the trunk, one deputy said, was "the hardest job I ever undertook. The lid practically flew back like a jack-in-the-box. It was just plain awful."

Official county physician John T. Davis—a general practitioner in Walhalla—and coroner Floyd Owens viewed the body on site before it was moved, still in the trunk, to Ansel Funeral Home for viewing by the coroner's jury. The newspaper described the difficulty of removing the clothes and how jurors had to rush outside for fresh air.

Dr. Davis said Dover had been struck once on the left back of his head and had likely died instantly.

Lillian said Dover had thrown a hammer at her and threatened to kill her and her "semi-invalid" grandmother because they wouldn't give him money for more whiskey. She admitted she hit him with a double-sided axe, but she hadn't meant to hurt him, only to scare him enough to protect her and her grandmother. She said he'd been on a binge for three days, and he could be a nasty drunk.

Lillian told police the incident happened outside, near the woodpile. Her grandmother said it happened in the house, and when deputies found a large bloodstain hidden under a linoleum rug in the house, Lillian admitted it was in that spot.

Asked about Dover's wallet and money, Lillian guessed he'd spent all his money on whiskey, but she didn't know where his wallet was. She'd given it to him for his last birthday. The wallet was never found.

In the days before the death was discovered, a taxi driver gave Lillian a ride to town, where she bought groceries and the linoleum rug. She later admitted she wanted the rug because she "couldn't stand the looks of that blood." The driver testified he'd left her packages on the porch and hadn't entered the house. The same taxi driver took her to Seneca when she went looking for a minister.

Inconsistencies about how events unfolded and how Lillian had gotten Dover into the trunk and hidden his body led investigators to Olin Crowe, a thirty-three-year-old friend of Lillian's. The two had been keeping company for about a year, though Crowe, a loom fixer at Chicopee Mill, was married and lived in the Flat Shoals area with his wife and six children.

Olin Crowe admitted he'd come to pick Lillian up several times, but he'd never been in the house. He would pick her up at a bridge behind the house because he and Dover, who happened to be his cousin, had words a couple of months before about him dating Lillian. The day Crowe took Lillian to Walhalla to have a tooth pulled, she told him Dover had gone missing. She seemed more puzzled than worried, he said.

Lillian had confessed to the preacher that she'd been seeing a married man, "but there had never been anything between them." Asked how Dover treated her, she testified "sometimes he couldn't have been better, but other times was mean." She was in love with Crowe. "He asked nothing of me and made no promises. To me that was a lot to be thankful for."

The coroner's jury held Lillian Thrasher for the grand jury. After Crowe was charged with murder and released on a $4,000 bond, Lillian then made a second statement to the sheriff, saying Crowe was the one who struck the fatal axe blow and that he forced her to help him hide the body in the trunk and threatened to kill her if she said anything.

The case held such interest that the slightest incident made news. The pastor's family had taken Lillian to live with them. In April, two months after the killing, the story of Lillian and the pastor's children going to the hospital for what was likely a stomach bug made the front page. When the pastor's house was broken into during Easter church services, that, too, made the front page. The wedding ring Lillian said Crowe gave her was stolen. Even more inexplicably, a card she said came from Dover's missing wallet was left on the kitchen counter.

In 1957, county courts wasted no time in bringing criminal cases to trial. Less than five months after her confession, Lillian Thrasher's trial started in the Oconee County Courthouse. On Friday, the second day of the two-day trial, she pleaded guilty to lesser charges of accessory after the fact of murder and desecration of the dead.

Judge J.B. Pruitt sentenced Lillian to the state's Industrial School for Girls until she turned twenty-one and no sooner, a term of three and a half years. He noted her father was in the penitentiary, her mother's whereabouts were unknown and she hadn't had the opportunity to lead a normal life. "The situation under which you have lived is deplorable. Of course," he said, "there may not be much to you anyway, but now time will tell."

After her sentencing, Lillian ran to hug the pastor's wife.

Right: The murder trials of Lillian Thrasher and Olin Crowe were held in this now-abandoned Oconee County Courthouse. *Photo by Cathy Pickens.*

Below: Chicopee Manufacturing rehired Olin Crowe when he was released from prison. *Photo courtesy of Chicopee collection.*

Crowe's two-day trial began immediately. Lillian, who hadn't testified at her own trial, was the chief witness against Crowe. She denied her earlier statements that she'd done the killing and instead testified that Crowe forced her to help clean up.

Crowe's wife testified she'd washed her husband's clothes and saw no blood on them. Several witnesses debated the details of the search for Dover and where Crowe was seen. After five early-morning hours of deliberation, the jury acquitted Crowe on the murder charge but found him guilty of the accessory and desecration charges.

For the Monday morning sentencing, the courthouse was again packed, though the crowds dwindled when the announcement didn't come quickly. The judge gave Crowe a six-year sentence, with an additional two years for statutory rape, given Lillian's youth. But the judge said he would hear arguments on Thursday about whether the sentence was too severe.

Crowe began his sentence at the Oconee prison camp. He was eventually released and returned to his job at Chicopee Mill. Lillian disappeared from the news.

Shortly after the murder, Ethel Vaughn, Lillian's grandmother, went to live in the county home. The old farmhouse was torn down.

Visiting Mummy

While South Carolina seems to lack any mummies of its own, the Upstate did enjoy a visit from one of the country's most famous traveling mummies: Marie O'Day and her Palace Car. A small note in the April 14, 1954 *Keowee Courier* announced that the Walhalla Fire Department would sponsor a display on Main Street of "a modern $10,000 automobile van" carrying the mummified body of "a murdered Salt Lake City night club dancer."

Though patrons still visit mummies of historic and scientific significance in museum displays, the age of traveling mummies vanished with carnival freak shows. But for a time, to draw crowds willing to plunk down coins to see a show, a series of industrious promoters gave Marie a backstory sure to enthrall. According to the bills promoting her appearances, Marie had been a stripper or a showgirl in Salt Lake City in 1925. That is, until a jealous boyfriend or husband stabbed her, slit her throat and threw her in the Great Salt Lake, where she floated for twelve years—her body, even her red hair, completely preserved.

In 2002, two professors from Quinnipiac University and the *National Geographic* channel's "The Mummy Roadshow" studied Marie's remains at Wilson Medical Center in North Carolina. Their CT scans and X-rays indicated her real story wasn't one that would draw sideshow crowds. Marie likely died of tuberculosis and was embalmed with arsenic, a technique with remarkable preservative properties used during the Civil War to enable families to return their loved ones back home from distant battlefields. Sadly, the traveling mummies were most often those without loved ones who could afford the embalming bill, so the undertaker would sell them to traveling showmen.

THE DARING DUMP TRUCK ESCAPE

In 1991, Oconee County had its own celebrated jail escapee.

Doyle Arthur Cannon was incarcerated in the Oconee County Detention Center for killing a man in a knife fight—he said it was self-defense. On May 14, while on a prison work detail near Salem, he was sent to pick up a load of gravel. He climbed into the county dump truck and simply drove away. Although he likely would've been granted parole at his next hearing in less than a year, he'd recently heard his wife was leaving him for another man, so maybe playing by the rules just didn't make sense anymore.

The dump truck alone wouldn't have earned him a mention in *TIME* magazine or an Associated Press release, but his repeated close escapes from as many as one hundred searchers with helicopters and bloodhounds just got more entertaining with each passing month. Doyle became something of a folk hero, complete with T-shirts, a ballad and an invitation to be grand marshal of the July Fourth Hillbilly Festival in Mountain Rest.

Those in Oconee County who found it humorous were quick to say they didn't condone that he'd killed a man, but even the director of the law enforcement center said, "He's a hard-working guy and I'd like to see him turn himself in. I'd hate to see him spoil his good record."

Things got serious when fifteen of Doyle's family members—including his seventy-year-old mother—were arrested for aiding him. In July, he was captured while mowing the lawn at a house near Central, South Carolina. He'd been staying in Liberty with a family who thought he was from Texas.

The *Keowee Courier* reported that some in Salem were saying if he'd been using a riding lawn mower instead of a push mower, he could've gotten away.

REFERENCES

Chapter 2: The Poisoners

Blum, Deborah. "The Imperfect Myth of the Female Poisoner." *Wired*, January 28, 2013. https://www.wired.com/2013/01/the-myth-of-the-female-poisoner/.

Johnston, Joni E. "A Psychological Profile of a Poisoner." *Psychology Today*, July 12, 2012. https://www.psychologytoday.com/us/blog/the-human-equation/201207/psychological-profile-poisoner.

Sharpe v. Sharpe, 416 S.E.2d 215 (S.C. 1992).

Smith v. Smith, 9 S.E.2d 584 (S.C. 1940).

State v. Griffin, 124 S.E. 81 (S.C. 1924).

The Eyedrop Murder

Allen, Karma. "South Carolina Woman Allegedly Killed Husband by Putting Eye Drops in Drinking Water." *ABC News*, September 3, 2018. https://abcnews.go.com/US/south-carolina-woman-allegedly-killed-husband-putting-eye/story?id=57569221.

Dys, Andrew. "SC Woman Pleads Guilty in Husband's Visine Poison." *Charlotte Observer*, January 17, 2020, 10A.

"Everyone's Favorite Uncle." *American Monster*, season 6, episode 1. Aired December 6, 2020.

Van Sant, Peter. "S.C. Nurse Who Fatally Poisoned Husband with Eye Drops: 'I Just Wanted Him to Suffer.'" *CBS News*, March 13, 2021. https://www.cbsnews.com/news/lana-steve-clayton-eye-drop-poison-suffer-48-hours/. For transcript, see also, "The Eye Drop Homicide." *48 Hours*, aired March 13, 2021. https://www.cbsnews.com/video/the-eye-drop-homicide/#x.

The Mensa Murder

Emsley, John. *The Elements of Murder: A History of Poison.* Oxford University Press, 2005.

Good, Jeffrey, and Susan Goreck. *Poison Mind.* New York: William Morrow, 1995.

McLeod, Mike. "Murder, He Wrote." *Orlando Sentinel,* May 12, 1991. https://www.orlandosentinel.com/news/os-xpm-1991-05-12-9105101101-story.html.

"Report Finds Flaws at FBI, but No Perjury." *CNN.com,* April 15, 1997. http://www.cnn.com/US/9704/15/fbi.crime.lab.update/.

Trepal v. Florida, 684 F.3d 1088 (11th Cir. 2012).

Trepal v. State, 621 So.2d 1361 (Fla. 1993).

Trepal v. State, 846 So.2d 405 (Fla. 2003).

CHAPTER 3: PRISON FLY-OUT

Alongi, Paul. "Prison Helicopter Escapee Dies." *Greenville News,* September 9, 2002, B1.

Herbert, David Gauvey. "The Ballad of Ron and Dorinda." *Esquire,* December 2020, 78.

Kulmala, Teddy. "Riots, a Bomb and a Helicopter Escape: 6 Big Stories from SC prisons." *The State,* April 19, 2018. https://www.thestate.com/news/local/crime/article209222199.html#storylink=cpy.

"Neighbor Says He Unwittingly Helped Woman Accused of Chopper Escape." *AP News,* December 21, 1985.

"Subjects Take Different Views of Movie Based on Escape." *Spartanburg Herald-Journal,* February 16, 1989.

Yenkin, Jonathan. "Women Linked by Copter Escapes." *Greenville News,* November 18, 1986, 9.

CHAPTER 4: NEW COLD CASE TECHNOLOGY

Gilreath, Ariel. "Murderer in 28-Year-Old Cold Case Identified through Genealogy Service." *Greenville Journal,* October 5, 2018. https://greenvillejournal.com/news/greenville-police-murderer-in-28-year-old-cold-case-identified/.

Gross, Daniel J. "Daughter of Serial Killer, Rapist Tied to 1990 Murder Speaks." *AP News,* January 19, 2019. https://apnews.com/article/26d01adbde1c458ab3d254d01183a255.

"The Hunt for the Runaway Killer." *The Genetic Detective,* season 1, episode 2. First aired June 2, 2020, on ABC.

Sederstrom, Jill. "Murder Suspect's Body Exhumed to Solve Two 1990s Cold Cases." October 8, 2018. https://www.oxygen.com/crime-time/murder-suspects-robert-brashers-body-exhumed-solve-two-1990s-cold-cases.

Chapter 5: Two Little Boys

Chuck, Elizabeth. "Susan Smith, Mother Who Killed Kids: 'Something Went Very Wrong That Night.'" *NBC News*, July 23, 2015. http://www.nbcnews.com/news/us-news/susan-smith-mother-who-killed-kids-something-went-very-wrong-n397051.

Henderson, Gary. *Nine Days in Union: The Search for Alex and Michael Smith*. Spartanburg, SC: Honoribus Press, 1995.

Morelli, Ricki. "Inside the Mind of Susan Smith." *Charlotte Observer*, July 22, 1995, 1A.

Pickens, Cathy. "The Heartbreaking Case of Susan Smith and the Death of Her Two Boys: A First-Person Account from the Courthouse Steps." *CrimeBeat*, June 7, 2021. https://medium.com/@cathypickens.

Rekers, George. *Susan Smith: Victim or Murderer*. Lakewood, CO: Glenbridge Publishing, 1996.

Russell, Linda H., with Shirley Stephens. *My Daughter Susan Smith*. Brentwood, TN: Authors Book Nook, 2000.

Smith, David, with Carol Calef. *Beyond All Reason: My Life with Susan Smith*. New York: Kensington Books, 1995.

Williams, Keira V. *Gendered Politics in the Modern South: The Susan Smith Case and the Rise of a New Sexism*. Baton Rouge: Louisiana State University Press, 2012.

Chapter 6: The Lady Killers

Sue Logue

Boswell, Charles, and Lewis Thompson. "Mayhem at Meeting Street." In *Harvesters of Murder*, 175–92. New York: Collier Books, 1962.

Dorn, T. Felder. *The Guns of Meeting Street*. Columbia: University of South Carolina Press, 2001. A thoroughly readable, well-researched account of the families, the region and the case.

Henderson, Gary. "Legacy of Hate: Family Feud Ends in 8 Deaths." *Spartanburg Herald-Journal*, February 5, 1995, 1A.

State v. Bagwell, 23 S.E.2d 245 (1942).

State v. Logue, 28 S.E.2d 788 (1944).

Sandra Beasley/Frances Truesdale

Curtis, Kim. "Victim's Widow Is Indicted: Frances Truesdale to Be Tried for Murder." *AP/York Observer*, April 21, 1996.

Denton, James. "Young Says Farewell." *Blythewood Online*, July 25, 2014. https://www.blythewoodonline.com/2014/07/young-says-farewell/.

Holland, Jesse J. "After Nearly 30 Years, Wife Convicted in Her Husband's Shooting Death." *AP News*, November 20, 1996. https://apnews.com/article/dfd1f33edf24b1e054c600c19ecd685c.

Smith, Benjamin H. "Two-Time Widow Guns Down Husbands Decades Apart." *Oxygen Crime News*, October 9, 2019. https://www.oxygen.com/snapped/crime-time/frances-truesdale-murder-two-husbands.

Truesdale v. Commonwealth, Record No. 1423-92-3 (Va. Ct. App. May 17, 1994). https://casetext.com/case/truesdale-v-commonwealth-1423-92.

Chapter 7: The Murder of Faye King

Charlotte Observer coverage of Chester County trial, July 1–12, 1929, 1A.

Gardner, Miles. *Further Tales of Murder & Mayhem in Lancaster, Kershaw, and Chesterfield Counties.* Spartanburg, SC: The Reprint Company, 2006.

Quinn, Sheriff Fred E., as told to C.R. Sumner. "Faye King—Poisoned or Strangled—Which?" *True Detective Mysteries*, December 1931, 38–43, 83–85.

State v. King, 155 S.E. 409 (S.C. 1930).

Chapter 8: The Witch Trials

"The Fairfield Witch Persecution of 1792." Fairfield County Historical Museum, October 18, 2017. https://www.facebook.com/201196703322943/posts/the-fairfield-county-witch-persecution-of-1792everyone-has-heard-of-the-salem-ma/1343772952398640/.

Gandee, Lee R. "The Witches of Fairfield, S.C." *Fate*, January 1970, 36. Republished in Esoterica Columbia blog, July 30, 2016. http://esotericcolumbia.blogspot.com/2016/07/the-witches-of-fairfield-sc.html.

"A History of Saxe-Gotha Township." https://www.carolana.com/SC/Towns/Saxe_Gotha_Township_SC.html.

Lake, William G. "Witchcraft in South Carolina." *The South Carolina Magazine*, June 1952. https://dspace.ychistory.org/bitstream/handle/11030/71368/00001344.pdf?sequence=1.

Moore, Peter N. "Religious Radicalism in the Colonial Southern Backcountry." *Journal of Backcountry Studies*, Vol 1:2, 2006, 1–19. http://libjournal.uncg.edu/jbc/article/view/48.

O'Neall, John Belton. *Biographical Sketches of the Bench and Bar of South Carolina.* Charleston: S.G. Courtenay, 1859. https://www.carolana.com/SC/eBooks/Biographical_Sketches_of_the_Bench_and_Bar_of_South_Carolina_Volume_I_John_B_O%27Neall_1859.pdf.

Woodmason, Charles. *The Carolina Backcountry on the Eve of the Revolution.* Richard J. Hooker, ed. Chapel Hill: University of North Carolina Press, 1953.

Chapter 9: The Highway 93 Murders

"Accused Strangler Arrested." *CBS News*, June 7, 2006. https://www.cbsnews.com/news/accused-strangler-arrested/.

"Authorities Release Incident Report in Bikini Strangulation Case." *Fox News*, May 31, 2006, updated January 13, 2015. https://www.foxnews.com/story/authorities-release-incident-report-in-bikini-strangulation-case.

Chandler, Ray. "Oconee Sheriff Launches Cold-Case Website." *Independent Mail* (Anderson, SC), May 23, 2013. https://archive.independentmail.com/news/oconee-sheriff-launches-cold-case-website-ep-361698941-347738641.html/.

"Cold Case: Clemson U Student Murdered After Going 4-Wheeling with Friends." *True Crime Daily*, March 29, 2016. https://truecrimedaily.com/2016/03/28/clemson-student-goes-out-for-4-wheeling-with-friends-never-returns/.

Field, Carla. "Task Force Hopes Suspect Profiles Will Help Solve 1997 Killing of Clemson Student." *WYFF 4*, February 17, 2017. https://www.wyff4.com/article/task-force-hopes-suspect-profiles-will-help-solve-1997-killing-of-clemson-student/8948732#.

"Golden Sentenced to Life for 1988 Murder." Tenth Circuit Solicitor (SC), December 18, 2008. https://www.solicitor10.org/2008/12/18/golden-sentenced-to-life-for-1988-murder/.

Gross, Daniel J. "Man on SC Death Row for Rape, Murder of Clemson Student to Be Re-Sentenced After 15 Years." *Greenville News*, May 28, 2020. https://www.greenvilleonline.com/story/news/local/south-carolina/2020/05/08/jerry-buck-inman-death-row-rape-murder-clemson-sc-student-re-sentenced/3088431001/.

Hester, Ashton. "March 6, 1968: Oconee Gives Up Fight; Clemson Lost Forever," in *Looking Back: 1938, 1948, 1958, 1988, 1998, 2008.* Xlibris, 2020.

Jackson, Vince. "Unsolved Murder of Clemson Student Will Haunt Police, Friends." *Independent Mail* (Anderson, SC), July 31, 2008. https://205guy.wordpress.com/tag/clemson-murders/.

State v. Inman, Final Brief of Respondent to S.C. Supreme Court, June 21, 2011. https://www.sccourts.org/caseofmonth/Sep2011/briefRespondent.pdf.

Chapter 10: The Random Killer

Gowdy, Trey. *Doesn't Hurt to Ask.* New York: Crown Forum, 2020.

Gulla, Tim. "Killer Granted New Sentencing Hearing." *Gaffney Ledger*, September 7, 2016.

Kroll, Andy. "The Endless Trial of Trey Gowdy's Benghazi Committee." *Rolling Stone*, January 14, 2016.

Maniloff, Randy. "Former US Rep. Trey Gowdy on Being a Prosecutor: 'That's the Job I Want to Be Known For.'" *ABA Journal*, September 15, 2020. https://www.abajournal.com/web/article/former-US-rep-trey-gowdy-talks-why-he-wants-to-be-known-as-a-prosecutor.

State v. Binney, SC S.Ct. Opinion No. 25920, filed January 10, 2005. https://www.sccourts.org/opinions/advsheets/no22005.pdf.

CHAPTER 11: THE SERIAL KILLERS

Greenville's Reedy River Killer

Moorefield, April E. "Families Hold Breath as Killer Up for Parole." *Greenville News*, October 8, 1997.

Riddle, Lyn. "Greenville Mom Fights Parole of Daughter's Killer." *Greenville News*, July 5, 2014. https://www.greenvilleonline.com/story/news/crime/2014/07/05/victims-mother-fights-parole-killer/12258635/.

Weimer, Carrie. "Family Asks for 19th Time That Parole Be Denied." *Fox Carolina News*, March 23, 2021. https://www.foxcarolina.com/news/family-asks-for-19th-time-that-parole-be-denied-for-man-who-brutally-killed-2/article_34bfc2da-8c1d-11eb-b58c-a7cb4823870e.html.

The Gaffney Killers

Bovsun, Mara. "Not So Peachy: South Carolina Town Has a Blood-Drenched History of Serial Killers." *New York Daily News*, September 16, 2018. https://www.nydailynews.com/news/ny-news-gaffney-serial-kilers-20180912-story.html.

DePriest, Joe, and Christopher D. Kirkpatrick. "Serial Killer Spent Last Days Partying/Motive for 5 Shootings Is Still a Mystery, Police Say." *Charlotte Observer*, July 8, 2009, 1A.

Gibbons, Bill R. *Martin: Profile of the Gaffney Strangler*. Privately published, 2003.

Holland, Jim, Jr. *A Reporter Remembers the Gaffney Strangler*. Gaffney, SC: Hometown Printing, 1981.

"Lock Up Your Daughters." *A Crime to Remember*, season 3, episode 1. Aired on November 10, 2015, on Investigation Discovery.

Martin, Tommy E. *"I Will Kill Again..." The Gaffney Strangler Story*. Cherokee Chronicle (Gaffney, SC), 1994.

Skipp, Catharine. "Kill and Kill Again." *Newsweek*, July 9, 2009. https://www.newsweek.com/gaffney-sc-haunted-murderous-memories-81707.

Todd Kohlhepp

Burns, Michael. "Mom of Accused Serial Killer Todd Kohlhepp: He 'Is Not a Monster'." *USA Today*, November 11, 2016. https://www.usatoday.com/story/news/nation-now/2016/11/11/south-carolina-killers-mom-explains-why-her-son-todd-kohlhepp-killed-woman-chained-dog-serial-killer/93640114/.

Douglas, John, and Mark Olshaker. *The Killer across the Table*. New York: HarperCollins 2019.

Hernandez, Nina. "Who Is Todd Kohlhepp, Accused South Carolina Serial Killer?" *Rolling Stone*, November 15, 2016. https://www.rollingstone.com/culture/culture-news/who-is-todd-kohlhepp-accused-south-carolina-serial-killer-118166/.

Serial Killer: Devil Unchained, Investigation Discovery, July 2019.

Smith, Tim. "As a Teen in Kidnapping Case, Kohlhepp Called 'Devil on a Chain.'" Greenville News, November 4, 2016. https://www.greenvilleonline.com/story/news/crime/2016/11/04/teen-kidnapping-case-kohlhepp-called-devil-chain/93311850/.

"Todd Kohlhepp: Confessions of a Suspected Serial Killer." *48 Hours*, November 12, 2016. https://www.cbsnews.com/news/todd-kohlhepp-case-48-hours-confessions-of-a-suspected-serial-killer-buried-truth/.

Chapter 12: Hometown Crimes

"Admits Killing Corbins." *The Watchmen & Southron* (Sumter, SC), July 10, 1909.

"The Ballad of Doyle Arthur Cannon." https://www.youtube.com/watch?v=3FXrWxSdB90.

"Cheek Charged with Murder of Neighbor," *Keowee Courier*, September 11, 1968.

Corbin murders and trial: *Keowee Courier*, March 10, 1909, and July 7, 1909 editions.

Dover murder and trial: *Keowee Courier*, February–July 1957.

Elrod v. Moss, 278 F.123 (4th Cir. 1921).

"Escaped Killer Becoming Folk Hero; 'Doyle-Watchers' Follow Exploits." *AP News*, July 15, 1991. https://apnews.com/article/99e1b7bf2a00fbaf98f3d72a85a2c50e.

Hester, Ashton. Doyle Arthur Cannon in "Observations and Meditations," Facebook, July 28 and August 4, 2021. https://www.facebook.com/ashton.hester.505.

"Marie O'Day." http://www.sideshowworld.com/76-Blow/Marie/Main/Page-O%27Day.html.

"Marie O'Day's Palace Car." *Keowee Courier*, April 14, 1954.

Oconee County coroner's inquest report: Oscar Dover, February 23, 1957.

Oconee County coroner's inquest report: Willie Underwood, October 24, 1968.

Smith, Fleming. "SC's Moonshine Culture and Its Long, Bullet-Riddled History." *Post and Courier*, January 10, 2020, updated January 21, 2021. https://www.postandcourier.com/news/scs-moonshine-culture-and-its-long-bullet-riddled-history/article_33cdd40e-1ac0-11ea-adc4-1fed09721275.html.

"South Carolina: A Cannon on The Loose." *TIME*, Monday, July 29, 1991. http://content.time.com/time/subscriber/article/0,33009,973469,00.html.

Stewart, Bruce E., ed. *King of the Moonshiners: Lewis R. Redmond in Fact and Fiction*. Knoxville: University of Tennessee Press, 2008.

ABOUT THE AUTHOR

C athy Pickens is a former lawyer and current crime fiction writer (*Southern Fried Mysteries*, St. Martin's/Minotaur), true crime columnist for *Mystery Readers Journal* and professor emerita in the McColl School of Business. She served as national president of Sisters in Crime and on the boards of Mystery Writers of America and the Mecklenburg Forensic Medicine Program (an evidence collection/preservation training collaborative).

She is also the author of *CREATE!* (ICSC Press), offers coaching and workshops on developing the creative process and works with writers on telling their stories.

Her other books from The History Press include: *Charleston Mysteries*, *Charlotte True Crime Stories*, *True Crime Stories of Eastern North Carolina* and *Triangle True Crime Stories*.

If you enjoyed this book, please consider posting a review on your favorite review site.